GCSE
Physical Education
The Revision Guide

This book is for anyone doing **GCSE Physical Education**.

GCSE PE is all about understanding how physical activity and your lifestyle can affect you and your body.

Happily this CGP book includes all the **PE facts** you need to learn for the exam. And in true CGP style, we've explained it all as **clearly and concisely** as possible.

It's also got some daft bits in to try and make the whole experience at least vaguely entertaining for you.

What CGP is all about

Our sole aim here at CGP is to produce the highest quality books — carefully written, immaculately presented and dangerously close to being funny.

Then we work our socks off to get them out to you — at the cheapest possible prices.

Contents

Published by CGP

Contributors:
Charley Darbishire, Mary Falkner, David Hickinson, Sharon Keeley, Simon Little,
Andy Park, Glenn Rogers, Caley Simpson, Sarah Williams.

ISBN: 978 1 84762 305 8

With thanks to Chris Cope, Gemma Hallam and Paul Jordin for the proofreading.

Definition of Health on page 1 © WHO 2008. All rights reserved. World Health Organisation
http://www.who.int/about/definition/en/print.html

Image on page 68 – © TM International Olympic Committee – All rights reserved.

Printed by Elanders Ltd, Newcastle upon Tyne.
Clipart from Corel®

Based on the classic CGP style created by Richard Parsons.

Photocopying more than one chapter of this book is not permitted. Extra copies are available from CGP.
0800 1712 712 • www.cgpbooks.co.uk

PE and Your Healthy, Active Lifestyle

The first stop on the PE fun bus — competence, performance, creativity and health. These spring up everywhere in GCSE PE — so make sure you understand what each one means. Heeeeeeere we go...

You Need to be *Competent* and *Creative* to *Perform* Well

1) You need to be competent to be able to do something successfully.

> COMPETENCE is the relationship between skill, and knowing how and when to use skills, tactics, strategies and compositional ideas. To be competent you need to be physically and mentally ready to do an activity.

So in rugby, being competent could mean using tactics like set plays. In dance, you need to know what ideas or emotions you're trying to get across through your movements.

2) To perform well you need to use your competencies.

> PERFORMANCE is using your physical competencies with your knowledge of a physical activity to produce an effective and successful result.

- In team sports, you need to use other people's strengths to help the team perform at its best — if someone's a great forward in football, it'd be silly to have them playing as a goalkeeper.
- To perform well, you need to know what counts as a success in an activity (e.g. scoring a goal) — otherwise you'll have no idea what you should be aiming to do.
- To perform better, you need to be able to analyse and evaluate your performance to see where you could improve.

3) Being creative can have huge advantages in all sorts of activities.

> CREATIVITY is where you explore and experiment with techniques, tactics and compositional ideas to produce successful results.

- Sometimes it's obvious when creativity is important, like in expressing and communicating ideas when choreographing a dance.
- Being creative also helps you try out different techniques and solve problems. Creative tactics are often the key to performing well.

Dave thought 'I'm a little teapot' was the height of creativity.

PE can Help you Lead a *Healthy, Active Lifestyle*

1) Most of us exercise just to stay fit and healthy, or just for fun.
2) Being healthy is more than just having a healthy body. Remember this definition of health — it's the one used by the World Health Organisation (WHO).

> Health is a state of complete mental, physical and social well-being, and not just the absence of disease and infirmity.

PHYSICAL WELL-BEING:

1) Your heart, kidneys, and the rest of your body are working well.
2) You're not suffering from any diseases or injuries.
3) You're not physically weak (infirm), so you can easily do everyday activities.

MENTAL WELL-BEING:

1) You don't have too much stress or anxiety.
2) You're not suffering from any mental illnesses.
3) You feel content.

SOCIAL WELL-BEING:

1) You have food, clothing and shelter.
2) You have friends.
3) You believe you have some worth in society.

Incompetent but creative — one out of three ain't bad...

Well... who knew there was so much more to being healthy than eating an apple a day? Learn the definition of health and remember it's made up of three parts — physical, mental and social well-being. Oh, and make sure you know what competence, performance and creativity are, they crop up all over the shop in PE.

Healthy, Active Lifestyles

Leading a healthy, active lifestyle isn't just a case of cutting down on the lard sandwiches, or moving from in front of the TV once in a while (but that sure can help)... everything you do affects your health.

Stay Healthy by Leading a Healthy, Active Lifestyle

1) Your lifestyle is the way you live your life. It's everything you do — including your work and hobbies.

> A healthy, active lifestyle adds to your physical, mental and social well-being.
> It includes doing exercise and physical activity on a regular basis.

2) For a healthy, active lifestyle — exercise and think PEASED.

P → **PERSONAL HYGIENE:** Keep yourself clean — it'll help you to avoid loads of diseases. It won't do your social life any harm, either.

E → **EMOTIONAL HEALTH:** Feeling good is important. Try to avoid too much stress and worry. This can be caused by friends and relationships as well as things like work.

A → **ALCOHOL / DRUG USE:** Misuse of substances can lead to poor health. That includes alcohol and tobacco. Even breathing in other people's smoke (passive smoking) can lead to health problems.

S → **SAFETY:** If you have a dangerous job or hobby, you're more likely to injure yourself. So use the proper safety equipment — and in sport, play by the rules.

E → **ENVIRONMENT:** Pollution can cause respiratory problems. Noise can cause stress and affect your sleep.

Studies have also shown the more access you have to green space like parks and gardens, the better your mental well-being is likely to be.

D → **DIET:** You need the right balance of nutrients so you can cope with your lifestyle (see p28-29).

3) Your job can have a big effect — manual jobs and ones where you have to be on your feet all day are more physically demanding than office jobs. Similarly, jobs based outdoors are usually more physically demanding than those indoors. Working outdoors rather than cooped up in an office can be good for your mental well-being too. Getting a physically active job will contribute towards a healthy, active lifestyle.

There are ways to Measure Health and Well-Being

You've probably got a good general state of health and well-being if:

1) You're satisfied and happy with the different parts of your life (work, home etc.).

2) You have positive feelings more often than negative ones i.e. you're happy most of the time. This is a sign of having good mental health.

3) You've got plenty of access to green space — the more access you have, the more likely you are to be healthy. (Not only are you more likely to have a place to do physical activity, but being outdoors is good for you mentally too).

4) You do a range of activities — the happier and healthier you are, the more likely it is you'll want to join in different activities.

Relax — it's part of a healthy, active lifestyle, you know...

All your lifestyle choices can affect your health. It's not just a case of doing some exercise and I'm alright (and healthy) Jack. Make sure you know the different things that make up a healthy, active lifestyle.

Healthy, Active Lifestyles

Doing exercise and physical activity is _good_ for you — that's not exactly a surprise. What is surprising is just how many _different ways_ it's good for you. And you get to learn them all... enjoy.

Physical Activity — _Any Form of Exercise or Movement_

1) Physical activity is just any form of exercise or movement.
   It can be planned and structured (like doing an aerobics class), or not (like dashing for the bus).
   In PE, you're normally interested in the structured and planned type.

> Exercise is any physical activity you do to improve or maintain your health and/or fitness.

It _doesn't_ have to be a _competitive sport_.

2) To stay healthy, you need to be physically active. You can increase the amount of physical activity you do by just changing a few habits — like walking or cycling to school instead of getting the bus.

Physical Activity has _Social_, _Physical_ and _Mental Benefits_

There's almost no end of good reasons for taking part in regular physical activity.

Social _Benefits_

1) FRIENDS — Doing physical activity can help you make friends with people of different ages and backgrounds. It might also just be a way of socialising with your current friends.

2) COOPERATION and TEAMWORK — By taking part in team activities like football, you have to learn how to cooperate and work with other people.

Physical _Benefits_

1) HEALTH — You can maintain or improve your health with regular physical activity. You reduce your chances of getting ill, and can increase your life expectancy.

2) FITNESS — You can increase or maintain your strength, endurance, flexibility and overall fitness (see p19).

3) PERFORMANCE — The more you do an activity, the better you'll get at it.

Mental _Benefits_

1) FEEL GOOD — As you do physical activity, your body releases more of a hormone called serotonin into your blood stream. Serotonin makes you feel happy — the higher your serotonin levels, the happier you feel.

2) STRESS RELIEF — Doing physical activity can help relieve stress and prevent stress-related illnesses.

3) SELF-ESTEEM — taking part in a physical activity can improve your self-image, self-esteem, confidence, and generally make you feel better about yourself.

4) COMPETITION and PHYSICAL CHALLENGE — Whether you're in a competition, or just trying to better your last performance — physical activity can challenge you and drive you to do the best you can. It can also improve how you think and act under pressure.

5) ENJOYMENT — you might choose to do a certain activity because you enjoy it, whether you find it exciting or relaxing or somewhere in between.

Aesthetic Appreciation — _How Good an Activity Looks_

If you do an activity, you get a better understanding of it and the techniques involved. You also know what to watch out for, whether it's a great pass in football, or a punch combination in boxing. Having done the physical activity, you'll probably appreciate it more than someone who hasn't.

Phwoarr... did you see the way that frisbee glided?

Social, physical and mental... sounds like the Krypton Factor to me. Remember — physical activity is good for your body, mind and your ability to make friends even when sweaty. Make sure you know whether each benefit is social, mental or physical — it could be worth a tasty extra mark in the exam.

Roles in Sport

An <u>active participant</u> is anyone who takes part in a sport — but that doesn't just mean a player, oh no. There are loads of <u>different roles</u> in sport to take your pick from — and they all need <u>different skills</u>. <u>Improving</u> each set of skills is the main <u>benefit</u> of doing each role.

Players Perform and Organisers, well, Organise...

PLAYER/PERFORMER — someone who plays a sport or performs an activity

1) You normally become a player or performer because you <u>enjoy</u> doing a particular activity.

2) You get to have <u>fun</u>, and by <u>doing well</u> in the activity you get to <u>feel good</u> about yourself. You can also develop skills to <u>improve your performance</u>.

3) You need to be able to <u>listen</u> and <u>respond</u> to what your coach or team captain says, be able to <u>cooperate</u> and work with your <u>team</u>, and abide by the activity's <u>rules</u>.

4) You also need to be able to <u>adapt</u> to situations e.g. needing to change tactics during a tennis match.

ORGANISER — a player or non-player who brings together everything you need, when you need it

1) Organisers <u>arrange</u> and <u>coordinate</u> competitions and events, and organise <u>people</u> (players, officials, volunteers, etc.), <u>facilities</u> (e.g. booking pitches for practice sessions) and <u>time</u>. Being an organiser can also involve <u>supervising</u> other people, and <u>delegating</u> tasks (giving them out to other people).

2) A good organiser will show <u>initiative</u> and have a fine eye for <u>detail</u>. They can do wonders for <u>promoting</u> an <u>event</u>, <u>team</u> or <u>performance</u> — leading to <u>more people</u> coming to <u>watch</u> or <u>take part</u>.

3) By getting the <u>right people</u> in (e.g. top dancers) they can make sure they put on the best performance.

4) Being an organiser is a great way to stay involved in sport if you <u>can't participate</u> (e.g. through injury).

A Choreographer is the Designer of a Performance

<u>Choreographers design</u> and <u>arrange</u> staged performances — e.g. ballet.

1) Choreography is all about letting your <u>creative juices</u> flow by finding ways to <u>express an idea</u>.

2) A good choreographer can provide <u>exciting ideas</u> for dancers to work with.

3) Choreographers also have to <u>evaluate</u> dancer performance, and <u>communicate</u> with and <u>advise</u> performers on how to <u>improve</u> their individual and group performances.

All Sports need Officials

1) <u>Referees</u>, <u>officials</u> and <u>umpires</u> are the people who <u>control</u> what's going on in an activity.

2) They need to <u>know the rules</u> of their sport inside out, and have to be <u>observant</u> and <u>decisive</u> (as they often need to make decisions <u>quickly</u>).

3) They need to be <u>authoritative</u> and <u>confident</u> so they can keep <u>control</u> of the game. Once they've made a decision they need to be confident enough to <u>enforce</u> it even if players try and argue.

4) They're also responsible for checking the <u>equipment</u>.

By officiating, you can <u>improve</u> your knowledge of the <u>rules</u> of a game. It's also another role that lets you <u>take part</u> in an activity when you're <u>unable to play</u>.

There's no 1 in team... or referee... or sausage...

So, you don't actually need to do any running round and getting out of breath to be involved in sport. You can take part by organising a run (<u>organiser</u>), by telling people to run round expressing the feelings of a chicken on a hot day (<u>choreographer</u>), or by showing people a red card for not doing it properly (<u>official</u>).

Roles in Sport

So, you've got some players and some organisers — now you need someone to train and lead them...

Coaches and Team Captains Need to be Leaders

To be a good team captain or coach, you need to be able to lead and influence a group.
You also need to be enthusiastic about your sport and able to motivate yourself and your team.

COACH — a non-player that's in charge of training a group or individual

1) Coaches need to be specialists in their sport so they can come up with training ideas and game-winning tactics. They're often ex-players or ex-performers who want to stay involved in their activity.

2) They need to keep up with changing trends in the game e.g. new styles of play in football, and adapt their training accordingly to help players improve, both individually and as a team.

3) They're responsible for making sure performers/players:
   - are in the correct mental state — when learning new skills and during a performance.
   - are in the correct physical state — that not only are they fit to perform (e.g. not injured), but they're in peak physical shape to perform at their best.
   - have the correct techniques and skills they need to perform well.
   - behave themselves and follow the rules within their sport or activity.

4) To help players and performers improve, they need to be able to set goals and monitor and evaluate performance. They also need to be able to communicate their advice clearly, both verbally and non-verbally (see p46), as well as listen and respond to the players.

CAPTAIN — a player that leads their team during a game

1) They should be highly skilled in their sport, and able to perform reliably under pressure. That way they can act as role models for the other members of their team.

2) They need to be decisive and adapt to situations during a game. E.g. cricket team captains have to decide how to arrange the fielders, and work out bowling tactics to try and beat the opposing team.

Captains also need to be organised — they're often responsible for arranging practice sessions and matches.

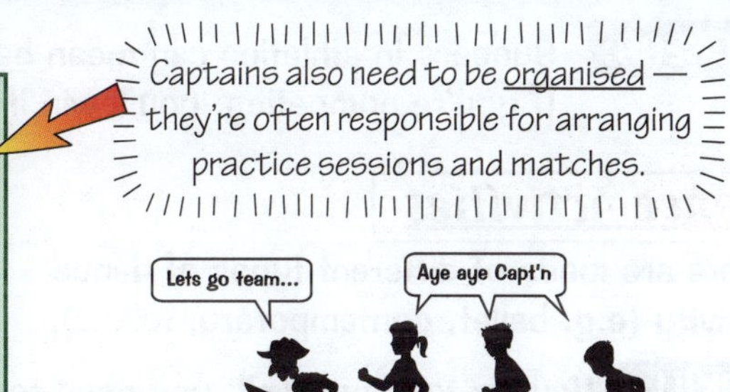

Volunteering — More Than a Nice Thing to Do

1) Being a volunteer means giving up your free time to do something without being paid. Sports volunteers can do anything from coaching, to driving the team minibus to matches, to washing the netball bibs.

2) Volunteers are really important in sport. Many sports clubs and initiatives are run by volunteers alone.

3) Volunteers need to be enthusiastic and able to work well as part of a team. Having leadership and problem-solving skills is always a bonus.

4) Yes, you have to work for free — but people usually get a lot back from volunteering. Helping people get into sport can be really satisfying. You can also make new friends, and improve your teamwork and leadership skills which are useful outside of sport.

5) It can also give you contacts which are really useful for getting more involved in sport. And the experience can make you generally more employable, too.

If only all coaches came with a TV, DVD player and air con...

My particular talent has always been making incredibly weak orange squash after a match. I always wondered why I was never made team captain, but now it all becomes clear. Make sure you know the qualities you need to be good in each role, as well as the benefits and reasons for doing each one.

Choosing a Physical Activity

There are loads of different physical activities to chose from — and they all need different skills. Improving skills is one of the benefits of sport — if there's one specific skill you want to develop, you might choose a sport for that reason. You need to know the following types of activities, the skills you need to do them, and what counts as a success in each one. If you're not doing the AQA course, you can just skip this page.

Different Types of Activity Require Different Skills...

Games Activities

Games (in PE... not the board or card sort) are any physical activities where you play against other people using a set of rules. E.g. football, rounders, cricket, basketball, badminton, squash...

SKILL: To perform well and win games activities, you need to be able to outwit and beat your opponents. E.g. changing the speed and spin of a cricket ball to bowl a batsman out.

SUCCESS: Success is beating your opponents in competition by affecting their performance. E.g. defending well in football so the opposite team are unable to score.

Athletic Activities

In athletics activities (e.g. high jump, 100 m sprint, archery...), you're judged on your performance in a particular activity. You can be either competing directly with other people, or with your previous best performance.

SKILL: In athletic activities, you might need jump the furthest, run the fastest, be the strongest, be the most accurate... you get the idea.

SUCCESS: Success in athletics can mean beating your personal best time, distance or score. If you're competing, you'll win if you get a better time or score than everyone else.

Gordon sets a new personal best for holding his breath.

Dance Activities

There are loads of different types of dance activity (e.g. ballet, contemporary, folk...).

SKILL: Usually to dance well, you need to be able to communicate particular ideas or emotions through your body movement. You need to get any technical dance steps right too.

SUCCESS: Success is being able to get across whatever ideas or feelings you or the choreographer intended to get across to an audience.

Gymnastic Activities

SKILL: In gymnastics, it's really important to be able to accurately copy actions and body movement sequences.

SUCCESS: Success in gymnastics is being able to repeat these movements as perfectly as possible. This could be in anything from a series of somersaults in a floor routine, to the correct movement on the rings.

Survival and Adventure Activities

SKILL: You need to be able to identify and solve problems to overcome challenges, e.g. finding hand holds in rock climbing.

SUCCESS: Success is managing to get over the challenges healthily and safely (and, obviously, surviving...).

Fitness and Health Activities

Fitness and health activities are activities that (unsurprisingly) improve your health and fitness e.g. aerobics.

SKILL: The skill in these activities is just to be able to safely and effectively exercise to improve your health.

SUCCESS: Improved fitness, health and wellbeing.

Skill: Juggling flaming knives — Success: not dying...

Phew — that was an action packed page to finish off the section. Now all you need to do is to learn the skills needed for each type of activity, and how to be successful in each one and the job's a good 'un.

Revision Summary — Section One

Woo... that's the first section over and wasn't it fantabulous? Not too long, not too short and full of facts about PE, lifestyles and roles in sport... I almost feel healthier just reading about it. But some of the topics in this section are a bit trickier than they look — they seem straightforward until you have to actually write about them. So, to make sure it's all as clear as mud and as memorable as errrm... that thing everyone always remembers, practise these questions. Keep going until you can get all of them right, first time, without having to peak back at the section.

1) What's the definition of competence?

2) What's the definition of performance?

3) How does being creative give you an advantage when you play sport?

4) Explain the meaning of:
   a) physical well-being,
   b) mental well-being,
   c) social well-being.

5) What do the letters **PEASED** stand for? Explain what each one means.

6) Access to green space is an indicator of good health and well-being.
   Give two other examples of how to measure health and well-being.

7) What's the definition of exercise?

8) Describe two social benefits of physical activity.

9) Describe three physical benefits of physical activity.

10) Describe five mental benefits of physical activity.

11) Explain what 'aesthetic appreciation' means.

12) What is the role of:
    a) a player/performer,
    b) an organiser.

13) Describe what a choreographer does.

14) What skills do officials need to be good at their role?

15) Explain what a coach does.

16) Explain the role of a captain.

17) Give two ways that volunteers help sport to take place.

18) Give two benefits of volunteering in sport.

19) For each of the following activities write down a skill associated with it and what counts as a success in that activity:
    a) games activities,
    b) athletic activities,
    c) dance activities,
    d) gymnastic activities,
    e) survival and adventure activities,
    f) fitness and health activities.

The Skeletal System

The skeleton gives the body its shape and has loads of jobs to do. It's made up of various kinds of bones, all meeting at joints that can move in different ways. Here's what you need to know...

The Skeleton has Different Functions

The skeleton does a lot more than you might think. The main functions are:

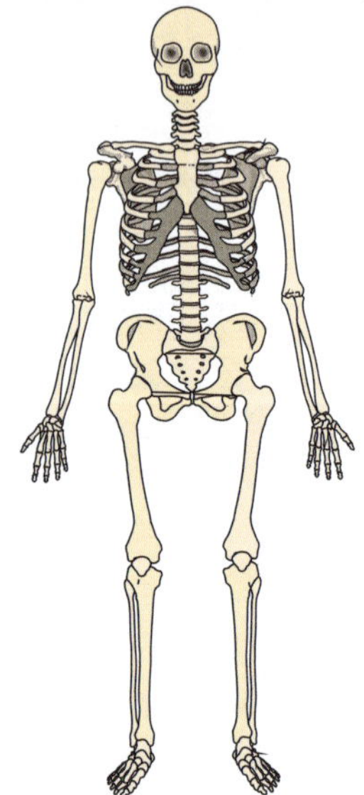

① **SUPPORT/SHAPE:**

1) The skeleton is a rigid bone frame for the rest of the body. Our shape is mainly due to our skeleton.
2) It's important to have a healthy posture, e.g. not slouching, to avoid problems like back pain.
3) The skeleton supports the soft tissues like skin and muscle.
4) Without the skeleton, we'd collapse like jelly.

② **PROTECTION:**

1) Bones are very tough.
2) They protect delicate organs like the brain, heart and lungs.

③ **MOVEMENT:**

1) There are loads of joints — places where two or more bones meet.
2) Muscles, attached by tendons, can move various bones.

④ **MAKING BLOOD CELLS:**

1) Long bones contain bone marrow.
2) New red blood cells are made in this bone marrow.
3) Red blood cells carry oxygen around the body (see p12) where it's used to release energy (see p13).

⑤ **MINERAL STORAGE:**

Bones store important minerals like calcium (see p29).

Connective Tissues Join Muscle and Bones

There are three types of connective tissue you need to know about.

CARTILAGE — forms cushions between bones to stop them rubbing.

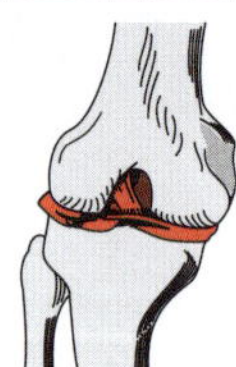

LIGAMENTS — like very strong string that holds bones together.

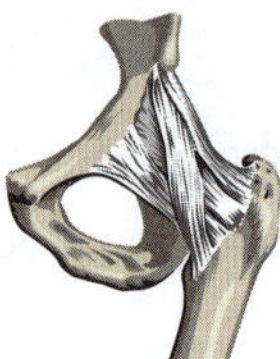

TENDONS — attach muscles to bones (or to other muscles).

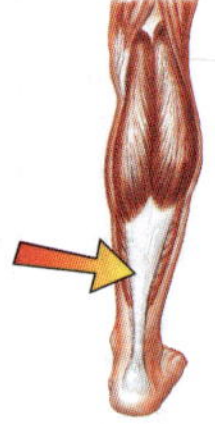

There are Two Different Types of Joint

There are two different types of joint that allow you to move:

1) **SLIGHTLY MOVABLE JOINTS**

Each of the bones rests on a cushion of cartilage...

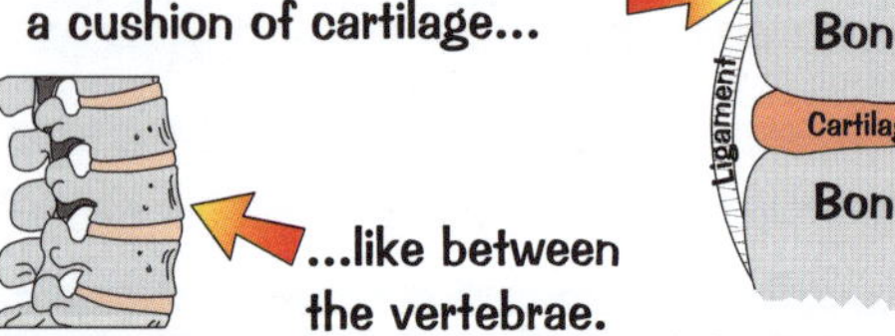

...like between the vertebrae.

The bones can move a little bit — but ligaments stop them moving too far...

2) **FREELY MOVABLE JOINTS**

These contain synovial fluid, which lubricates (or 'oils') the joint.

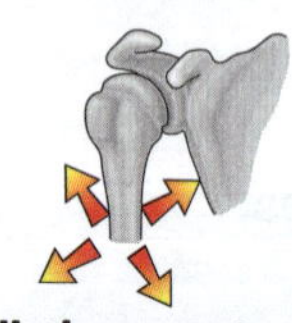

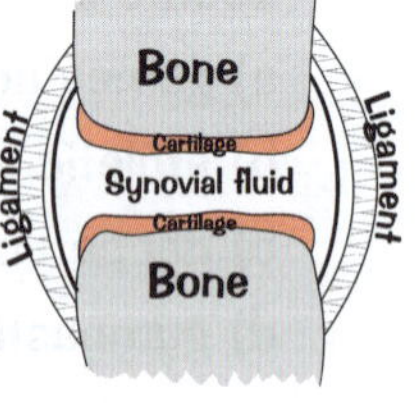

The shoulder joint is a freely movable joint.

All the moving parts are held together by ligaments.

All this talk about joints is making me hungry...

The skeleton is dead important. Imagine life without it — we'd all be wobbling about like blancmanges. You need to know what the skeleton does — so learn its five main functions. Also learn the names of the bits and pieces that make up your joints, as well as the stringy bits that hold the whole lot together.

The Skeletal System

Joints are <u>clever</u> old things — they let bits of your body move in certain directions. You'll need to know the <u>kinds of movement</u> your body can make and the <u>types</u> of joint too.

There are *Five Kinds* of Joint *Movement*

There are <u>five</u> different kinds of movement the joints can allow. You need to know the info.

| **EXTENSION** | **FLEXION** | **ADDUCTION** | **ABDUCTION** | **ROTATION** |

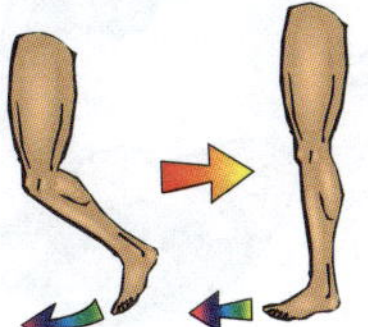 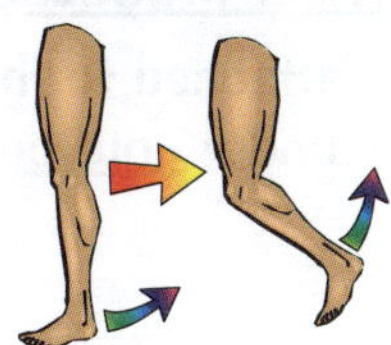   

<u>Opening</u> a joint.

<u>Closing</u> a joint.

Moving <u>towards</u> an imaginary <u>centre line</u>.

Moving <u>away</u> from an imaginary <u>centre line</u>.

<u>Turning</u> a limb <u>clockwise</u> or <u>anticlockwise</u>.

There are *Two Types* of *Freely Movable Joint*

Your shoulder and knee are both <u>freely movable joints</u> (see p8). But, your shoulder can move in more directions than your knee. That's because it's a <u>different</u> kind of freely movable joint.

There are <u>two types</u> you need to know about:

BALL AND SOCKET

1) Your <u>hips</u> and <u>shoulders</u> are ball and socket joints.
2) These joints can move in <u>all directions</u>, and they can <u>rotate</u> as well.
3) So this allows <u>flexion</u>, <u>extension</u>, <u>adduction</u>, <u>abduction</u> and <u>rotation</u>.

Actions where this type of joint is important:
<u>Shoulder</u> — bowling in cricket, arm swing in tennis.
<u>Hip</u> — any sort of running, kicking, doing the splits.

HINGE

1) Your <u>knees</u> and <u>elbows</u> are hinge joints.
2) The joint can go <u>backwards and forwards</u>, but not side-to-side.
3) This allows <u>flexion</u> and <u>extension</u>.

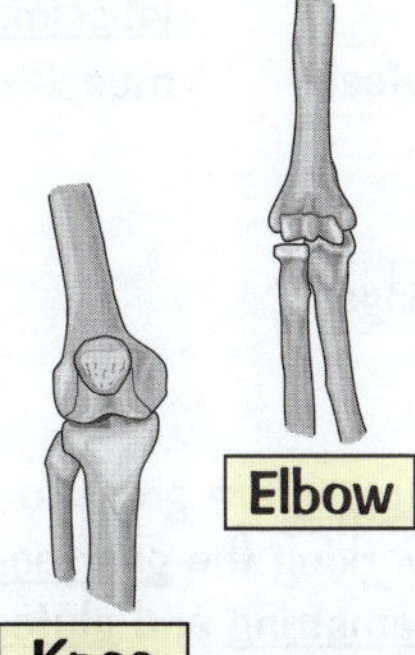

Activities where you have to <u>kick</u>, <u>run</u> or <u>throw</u> all use this joint. E.g. throwing a basket ball, kicking a football.

No bones about it — it's a humerus little page...

There's a load of niggly names to learn here — so give it some time. It can be a bit tricky, but try to think of ways to remember things. Like this: <u>ADDuction</u> is bringing two bits together, kind of like 'adding' them — while <u>ABDuction</u> is taking them away — like when you're <u>abducted by aliens</u>.

The Muscular System

There's lots to know about the <u>muscular system</u>. You need to know the two different <u>types of muscle</u>, and the <u>names</u> of the bigger, or more important, muscles. Here's everything you need...

There are *Two* Different *Types* of *Muscle*

1) Like the title says, there are <u>two different types of muscle</u> you need to know. These are...

INVOLUNTARY MUSCLES

Around <u>organs</u> such as the <u>intestines</u>, and <u>blood vessels</u>.

They work <u>without conscious effort</u> from you.

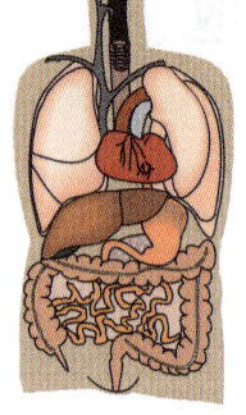

VOLUNTARY MUSCLES

They're attached to the <u>skeleton</u> and are under <u>your control</u>.

2) <u>All</u> muscles are made up of <u>fibres</u>.
3) <u>Nerve impulses</u> are what tell muscles to <u>contract</u> (or in the case of the heart, they cause it to contract in a regular pattern — the heartbeat).
4) Complex movements are made possible by the coordination of nerve impulses sent to the muscles by the <u>nervous system</u>.

Different Activities Work Different *Muscle Groups*

You need to know what the <u>big important muscles</u> are called. You also need to know which activities and movements are particularly good for each <u>muscle</u>. Luckily it's all in this lovely diagram — learn it well.

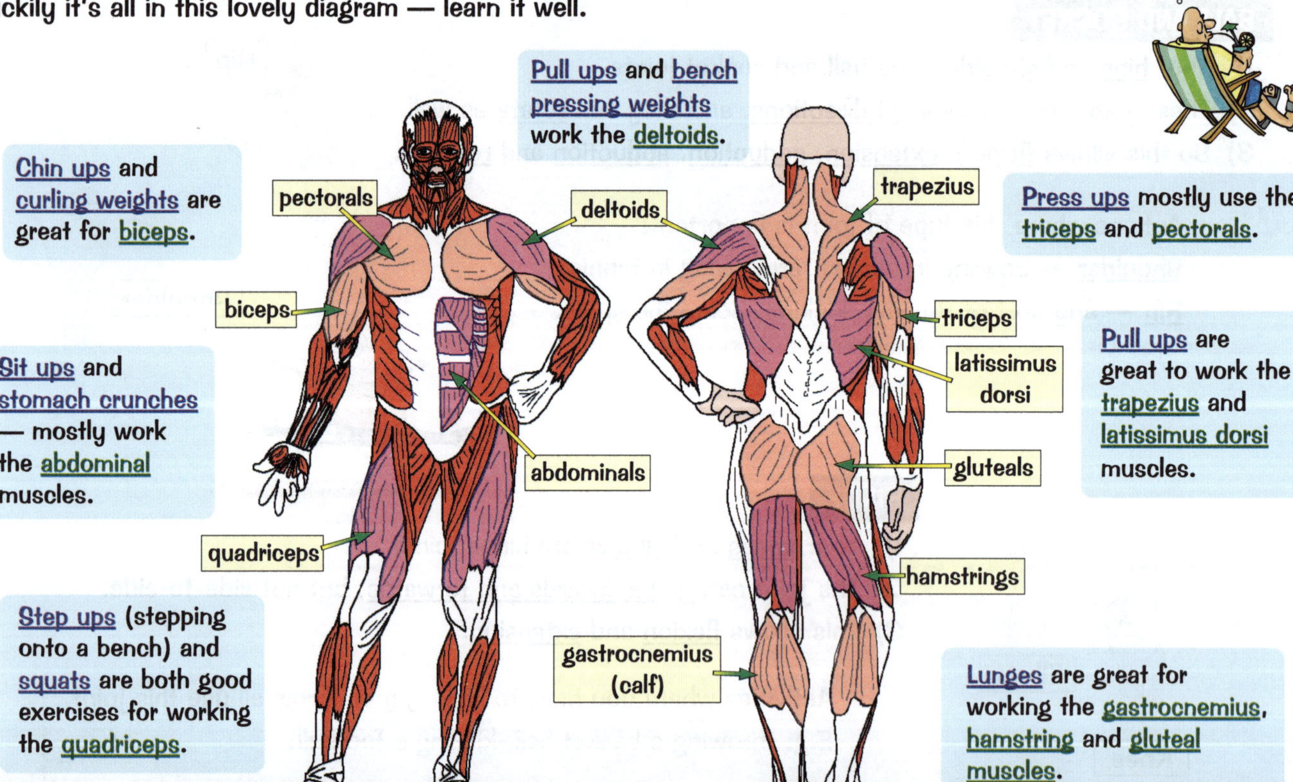

My muscles don't feel like they volunteer for anything...

OK, so there are quite a few big fancy words on that diagram, but I'm afraid you really do need to <u>know</u> the names of these muscles. It really can help to try and point at each one on your own body — but maybe not in public. Keep going 'til you can name them all without looking back at this page.

The Muscular System

You need to know that muscles work in <u>pairs</u>, and all the fancy names that go with it. There's a lot more that goes on for you to <u>flex your muscles</u> and show off your guns than you might think...

Muscles Pull on Bones

1) Muscles used for movement are attached to <u>two different bones</u> by <u>tendons</u>.
2) Only <u>one</u> of these bones will move when the muscle contracts.

> Muscles can only do one thing — <u>pull</u>.
> To make a joint move in two directions, you need <u>two muscles</u> that can pull in <u>opposite directions</u>.

Antagonistic Muscles Work in Pairs

1) <u>Antagonistic</u> muscles are <u>pairs of muscles</u> that work <u>against</u> each other.
2) One muscle <u>contracts</u> (shortens) while the other one <u>relaxes</u> (lengthens) and <u>vice versa</u>.
3) The muscle that's doing the work (contracting) is the <u>prime mover</u>, or <u>agonist</u>.
4) The muscle that's relaxing is the <u>antagonist</u>.
5) There are also muscles called <u>synergists</u>. They hold the stationary bone still, so only one bone moves
    — e.g. when the bicep contracts to bend the elbow, synergists stop the shoulder moving.

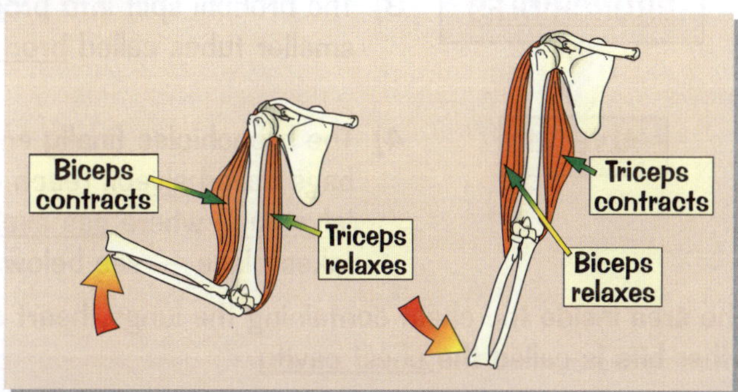

Your Muscles and Joints Act as Levers

Joints <u>multiply</u> either the <u>force</u> of a muscle, or the <u>speed</u> of a movement or both. When you bend your elbow, your muscles make a <u>short</u> movement, but your hand makes a <u>larger</u> one — this means your hand moves <u>more quickly</u>.

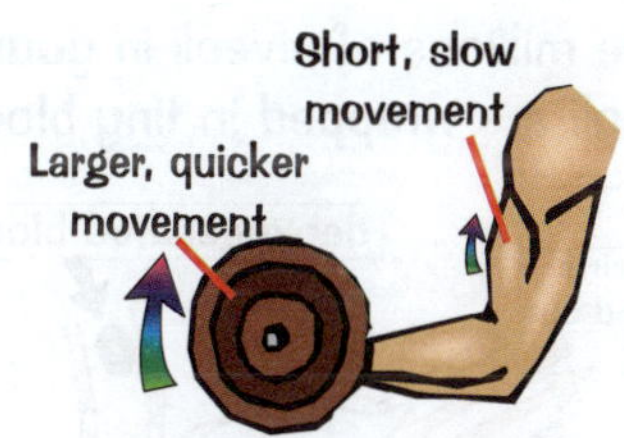

There are Two Types of Muscle Contraction

There are two types of <u>contraction</u> that a muscle can undergo — <u>isometric</u> and <u>isotonic</u>.

ISOMETRIC CONTRACTION — the muscle <u>stays the same length</u> and so nothing moves.
Like if you pull on a rope attached to a wall.

ISOTONIC CONTRACTION — the muscle <u>changes length</u> and so something moves.
Like if you exercise with weights that are free to move.

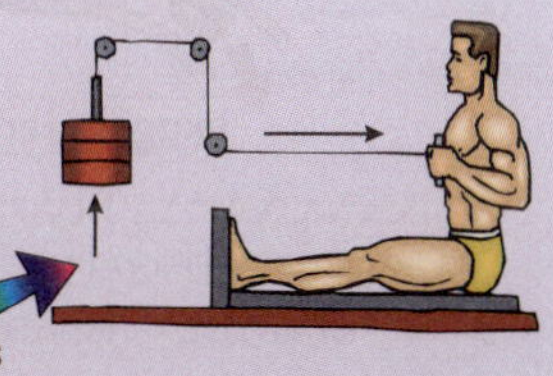

Moving joints — you'd better lever little space...

So muscles work in pairs — while one <u>contracts</u>, the other has a nice little <u>rest</u>. 'Antagonistic system' sounds pretty gruesome as well as being a pain in the er... arm. Don't panic — it's not too bad once you've read it through a few times. Make sure you learn all the names — oh, and all the other stuff too...

The Respiratory System

You'll probably recognise most of the stuff on this page from <u>biology</u> — but it's always good to have a recap. If you don't know this then stuff like 'how <u>smoking</u> affects <u>gas exchange</u> in the <u>alveoli</u>' on page 30 are just going to sound like complete gobbledy gook.

The **Air** You Breathe **Ends Up** in the **Alveoli**

The respiratory system is <u>everything</u> we use to <u>breathe</u>.

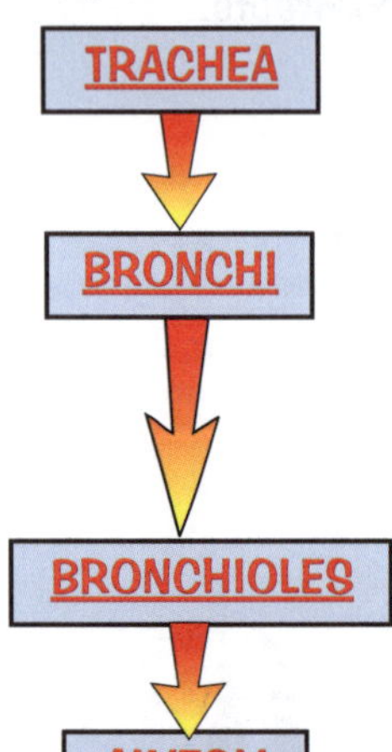

1) Air passes through the nose or mouth and then on to the <u>trachea</u>.

2) The trachea splits into two tubes called <u>bronchi</u> (each one is a '<u>bronchus</u>') — one going to each lung.

3) The bronchi split into progressively smaller tubes called <u>bronchioles</u>.

4) The bronchioles finally end at small bags called <u>alveoli</u> (each one is an '<u>alveolus</u>') where <u>gas exchange</u> takes place — see below.

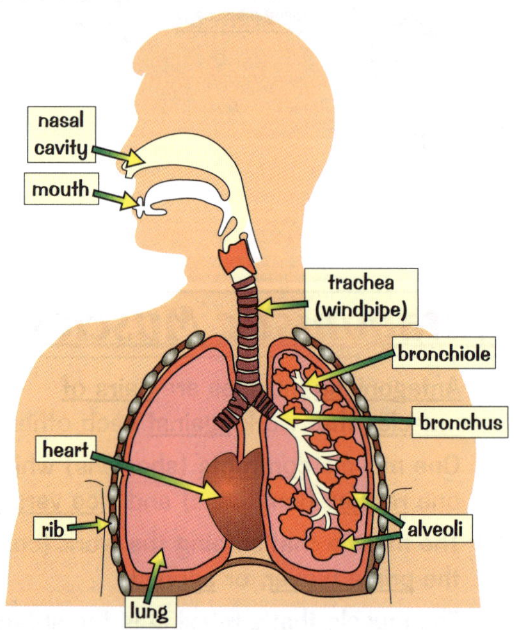

The area inside the chest containing the lungs, heart and all the other bits is called the <u>chest cavity</u>.

Oxygen and **Carbon Dioxide** are **Exchanged** in the Alveoli

There are millions of alveoli in your lungs. This is where the <u>gaseous exchange</u> happens. The alveoli are wrapped in tiny blood vessels called <u>capillaries</u>.

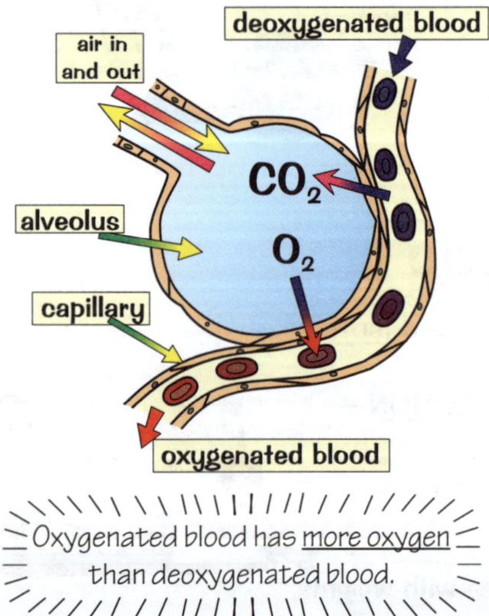

Oxygenated blood has <u>more oxygen</u> than deoxygenated blood.

When you breathe:

1) <u>Carbon dioxide</u> moves from your blood into the <u>alveoli</u>.

2) Oxygen in the alveoli moves across to the red blood cells. The red blood cells contain <u>haemoglobin</u>, which combines with the oxygen to make <u>oxyhaemoglobin</u>.

3) The red blood cells <u>carry</u> the oxygen around the body and <u>deliver</u> it to where it's needed.

4) At the same time, the blood <u>collects</u> carbon dioxide to be taken back to the lungs.

The air you breathe in and the air you breathe out are <u>different</u>. The air you breathe out has <u>less</u> oxygen, because the body's used some — but <u>more</u> carbon dioxide which is made during respiration (see p13).

Air we go — keeping trachea respiratory system...

This page is OK really — it's just got lots of tricky names that make it <u>seem</u> hard. Make sure you learn which gas goes where when you breathe, and what alveoli are. (Hint: alveoli are <u>not</u> a type of pasta.)

The Respiratory System

So, thanks to the lungs and red blood cells, oxygen can be moved round the body — great.
Now you need to know <u>why</u> we need that oxygen — enter <u>respiration</u>...

Aerobic Respiration — With Oxygen

1) <u>All</u> the living cells in your body need <u>energy</u>. Normally the body converts <u>glucose</u>
(a <u>sugar</u> found in food) into <u>energy</u> using <u>oxygen</u>. This is called <u>aerobic respiration</u>.

> Glucose + Oxygen ➡ Carbon dioxide + Water + Energy

2) If your body's keeping up with the <u>oxygen demand</u> of the cells, it means there's enough oxygen
available for aerobic respiration.

3) Activities where your body can <u>keep up</u> with
oxygen demand are called <u>aerobic activities</u>.

> **AEROBIC ACTIVITY:** 'with oxygen'.
> If the exercise you're doing isn't <u>too fast</u> and you're
> exercising at a <u>steady rate</u>, your heart and lungs can
> supply your muscles with all the oxygen they need.

4) You <u>breathe out</u> the carbon dioxide through
your lungs, while the water is lost as <u>sweat</u>,
<u>urine</u>, or in the <u>air</u> you breathe out.

5) As long as your muscles are <u>supplied with enough oxygen</u>, you can do aerobic exercise —
so this is used for <u>long periods</u> of exercise.

6) It's how <u>marathon runners</u> get their energy.

Anaerobic Respiration — Without Oxygen

1) During <u>vigorous exercise</u>, your body <u>can't</u> supply all the oxygen needed. When this happens,
your muscles release energy <u>without</u> using oxygen in a different process called <u>anaerobic respiration</u>.

> Glucose + No oxygen ➡ Lactic acid + Energy

2) Activities where your body has to do this are called <u>anaerobic activities</u>.

> **ANAEROBIC ACTIVITY:** 'without oxygen'. If you exercise in <u>short</u>, <u>fast spurts</u>, your heart
> can't supply your muscles with the blood and oxygen as fast as your cells use them.

3) The <u>lactic acid</u> produced in this process <u>builds up</u> after a while.

4) Lactic acid is a <u>mild poison</u> and its build-up soon makes your muscles feel <u>tired</u>
— so this form of respiration only works for <u>short</u>, <u>strenuous</u> activities.

5) To get rid of the lactic acid, you need <u>oxygen</u>. The amount of <u>oxygen</u> you need is
the <u>oxygen debt</u>. You breathe it in when you've stopped exercising so vigorously.

6) This is how <u>sprinters</u> get their energy.

Vital Capacity — The Most Air You Can Breathe In

1) When you breathe in and out normally, only a <u>small volume</u> of air moves in and out — the <u>tidal volume</u>.

2) You can use the tidal volume to work out the
'<u>minute volume</u>' — the amount of air inhaled in one minute.

> minute volume = tidal volume × respiratory rate

3) Your tidal volume is only a fraction of your <u>vital capacity</u>:

4) The <u>larger</u> your vital capacity, the <u>more oxygen</u> can be taken
in and absorbed into your blood stream in every breath —
so the oxygen supply to the muscles is increased.

> <u>VITAL CAPACITY</u> — the most air you could
> possibly breathe in after breathing out the
> largest volume of air you can.

Take a breather — there's a lung way to go yet...

<u>Aerobic</u> respiration is much more <u>efficient</u>, so the body uses it wherever it can. The trouble is, it's not fast.
If the body can't get enough oxygen, it has to use the <u>anaerobic</u> system and put up with the <u>lactic acid</u> for
as long as it can. Make sure you know all about <u>oxygen debt</u> and lactic acid, it's dead important.

The Cardiovascular System

Your cardiovascular system's made up of your <u>heart</u>, <u>lungs</u>, <u>blood</u> and <u>blood vessels</u> (<u>arteries</u>, <u>veins</u> and <u>capillaries</u>). You need to know what it does and how it does it...

The Cardiovascular System has Three Main Functions

1) **TRANSPORT** — <u>moving</u> things around the body in the bloodstream, like <u>oxygen</u>, <u>nutrients</u> (like glucose), <u>water</u> and <u>waste</u>.

2) **BODY TEMPERATURE CONTROL** — moving more blood nearer the skin <u>cools</u> the body more quickly. That's why your skin looks <u>redder</u> after exercise.

3) **PROTECTION** — moving <u>antibodies</u> around the body to fight disease. Your blood also <u>clots</u> to seal cuts.

Your Blood is made up of Cells, Platelets and Plasma

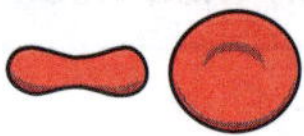

<u>RED BLOOD CELLS</u> — Carry oxygen around the body in red <u>haemoglobin</u>. They have <u>no nucleus</u>, leaving more space for haemoglobin.

<u>WHITE BLOOD CELLS</u> — Fight <u>against disease</u> by destroying bacteria, viruses and toxins. 

 <u>PLATELETS</u> — Small <u>fragments</u> of cells with <u>no nucleus</u>. They help blood to clot at wounds.

<u>PLASMA</u> — carries everything in the bloodstream. That includes blood cells, digested food (e.g. glucose), waste (e.g. urea, carbon dioxide) and hormones. 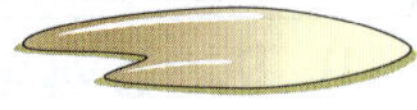

The Cardiovascular System Has a Double Circuit

1) The <u>cardiovascular system</u> is made up of three main parts — the <u>heart</u>, the <u>blood</u> and the <u>blood vessels</u>.

2) Each time blood goes right round your body, it goes <u>through the heart twice</u> — once through each side.

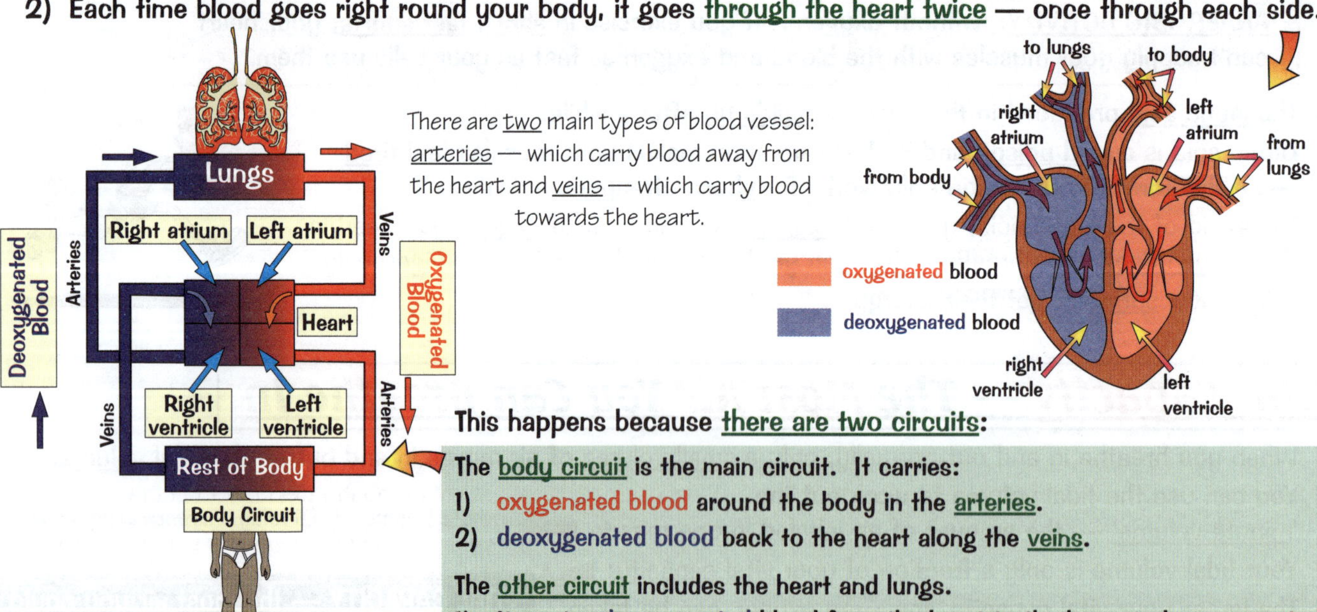

There are <u>two</u> main types of blood vessel: <u>arteries</u> — which carry blood away from the heart and <u>veins</u> — which carry blood towards the heart.

This happens because <u>there are two circuits</u>:

The <u>body circuit</u> is the main circuit. It carries:
1) oxygenated blood around the body in the <u>arteries</u>.
2) deoxygenated blood back to the heart along the <u>veins</u>.

The <u>other circuit</u> includes the heart and lungs.
1) It carries deoxygenated blood from the heart to the lungs to be oxygenated.
2) The blood then goes <u>back to the heart</u> to be pumped around the <u>body circuit</u>.

The heart — it's all just pump and circumstance...

Wow... and your cardiovascular system does all that without you even thinking about it. You know the drill, keep going over this page until you can scribble down all the facts blindfolded, while unicycling on a tight rope. OK, maybe just 'til you can do it without looking back at the page...

Exercise and the Cardiovascular System

When you start to <u>exercise</u>, your body has to make sure that your muscles get the <u>oxygen</u> they need so they can keep working. It also has to avoid <u>overheating</u>. It's all clever stuff.

Stroke Volume — Volume of Blood per Minute

1) Your <u>heart rate</u> is the number of times your heart beats <u>each minute</u>.

2) Your <u>stroke volume</u> is the amount of blood each ventricle pumps with <u>each contraction</u> (or heartbeat).

3) You can <u>multiply</u> your heart rate and stroke volume to work out the volume of blood pumped by a <u>ventricle per minute</u>. This is your <u>cardiac output</u>. There's more on heart rate on page 42.

HEART RATE	×	STROKE VOLUME	=	CARDIAC OUTPUT
HR	×	SV	=	CO

The Blood is Under Pressure

1) Every time your heart contracts, it <u>forces</u> blood around your body by <u>increasing</u> your <u>blood pressure</u>.

> BLOOD PRESSURE is the force caused by the blood on the walls of the blood vessels.

2) Your blood pressure <u>decreases</u> as it travels around each circuit — so the pressure in your <u>arteries</u> is <u>larger</u> than that in your <u>veins</u>.

<u>Arteries</u> have thicker and stronger walls than veins to cope with the higher pressure.

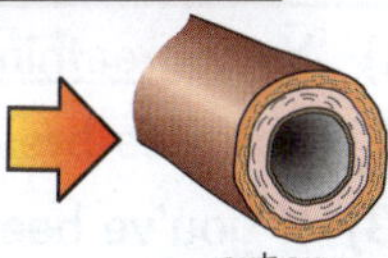

3) Blood pressure can be measured using a <u>sphygmomanometer</u>. It gives two readings:

(Possibly the most ridiculous word ever.)

> <u>SYSTOLIC PRESSURE</u> — the pressure of the blood in the arteries when the left ventricle <u>contracts</u>.
>
> <u>DIASTOLIC PRESSURE</u> — the pressure of the blood in the arteries when the left ventricle <u>relaxes</u>.

Your Body Moves Up a Gear When You Exercise

When you exercise, blood is <u>redistributed</u> around the body to <u>increase</u> the supply of <u>oxygen</u> to your <u>muscles</u> — this known as '<u>blood shunting</u>' or '<u>vascular shunting</u>'.

① When you exercise, your muscles start to <u>produce</u> more <u>carbon dioxide</u> and <u>need</u> more <u>oxygen</u>...

② ...so you start to <u>breathe</u> more <u>deeply</u> and <u>quickly</u>.

③ ...and your heart beats <u>faster</u> to <u>circulate</u> more oxygenated blood.

④ Your <u>arteries</u> widen to stop your blood pressure getting too <u>high</u>...

⑤ ...and to make the most of your <u>blood supply</u>, blood that would usually go to organs like the <u>gut</u> and <u>liver</u> is <u>shunted</u> to the <u>muscles</u>...

⑥ ...by blood vessels either widening (<u>vasodilation</u>) or constricting (<u>vasoconstriction</u>).

<u>Adrenaline</u> (a <u>hormone</u>) is released when you exercise, and causes changes 2 to 6.

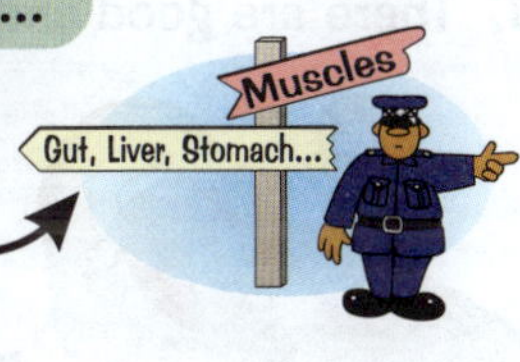

Ⓐ Also, as your muscles work, they generate <u>heat</u> — which warms your blood...

Ⓑ ...and this blood is <u>shunted</u> closer to your skin, so the heat can escape through <u>radiation</u>.

Which makes you go red.

Ⓒ And you also start to <u>sweat</u>, which helps keep you <u>cool</u>.

Get yourself in gear — or it could be embarrassing...

Blood shunting's <u>really</u> important. It's easier to remember it if you imagine yourself exercising — heart thumping, gasping for breath, red in the face, etc. It's also dead important that you learn about the '<u>shunt</u>' of blood towards <u>muscles</u> when you exercise. Know why and how it happens. It's amazing, I reckon.

Short-Term Effects of Exercise

During exercise, your <u>muscles</u>, <u>lungs</u> and <u>heart</u> all work harder. If you're doing the AQA courses you can skip the next couple of pages on the effects of exercise, and go straight on to the Revision Summary finale.

You Need to know the Short-Term Effects of Exercise

The Muscular System

1) Whatever type of exercise you do, your <u>muscles will contract</u> — either <u>isometrically</u> or <u>isotonically</u> (see p11).

2) As you exercise, the <u>temperature</u> of your muscles <u>rises</u>.

3) Your muscles work harder than usual during exercise, so they need <u>more energy</u>.

4) Your respiratory and cardiovascular systems quickly adapt to try to provide this — see below.

5) If your body can't keep up with the oxygen demand, your muscles will respire anaerobically (see p13) and produce <u>lactic acid</u>. If you use your muscles like this for long they feel <u>tired</u>. This is <u>muscle fatigue</u>.

The Respiratory System

1) Your <u>breathing rate increases</u> to increase your oxygen intake.

2) You also breathe <u>more deeply</u> than normal. This means you take in more oxygen with each breath.

3) If you've been doing <u>anaerobic activity</u>, your breathing rate and depth will remain high until you've taken in enough <u>oxygen</u> to 'pay off' your <u>oxygen debt</u>.

The Cardiovascular System

1) Just like your breathing, your <u>heart rate increases</u> to <u>increase</u> the blood supply to your muscles.

2) Your heart also <u>contracts more strongly</u> to pump even more blood around the body. This <u>increases</u> your <u>blood pressure</u>:

> The <u>more strongly</u> your heart <u>contracts</u>, the higher your <u>systolic</u> blood pressure will be. But your <u>diastolic</u> blood pressure usually stays the <u>same</u>.

3) Your heart rate will remain higher than normal until any <u>oxygen debt</u> is paid off.

Your Muscles Need to Rest and Recover after Exercise

1) After an exercise session, your muscles need time to <u>adapt</u> and <u>recover</u>.
2) If you don't rest for long enough, you could risk <u>injuring</u> yourself (see next page).
3) There are good and bad ways of <u>speeding up</u> the time it takes your muscles to <u>recover</u>...

DIET

Your muscles are made up of <u>proteins</u>. By eating a high protein diet, you can <u>speed up</u> the rate at which your body can <u>build</u> and <u>repair muscle</u> — <u>shortening</u> your <u>rest</u> and <u>recovery time</u>.

DRUGS

<u>Steroids</u> stimulate the body to produce muscle proteins at a faster rate. This also speeds up the time it takes to build and repair muscles.

Some athletes <u>illegally</u> use steroids so they can train harder and <u>improve</u> <u>their performance</u> (see p31).

My brainular system hurts...

After that brain workout, rest and recover with a nice cup of tea and a biscuit. Remember — exercise does more than just make you red faced and sweaty. You need to make sure you know all the <u>short-term effects</u> of exercise on each of your three main body systems. Next up, the long-term effects of exercise...

Long-Term Effects of Exercise

Exercising regularly makes your body more efficient and stronger, as well as helping to prevent nasty bone and joint problems. Remember, if you're doing the AQA course you don't need to know the stuff on this page.

Exercising Regularly has Many Long-Term Benefits

The Muscular System

1) Exercise and strength training make your muscles adapt — your muscle fibres get stronger and your muscle gets thicker. This thickening of muscles is called hypertrophy.

2) Your strength will increase — the thicker the muscle and the stronger the muscle fibres, the more strongly the muscle can contract.

3) Your tolerance to lactic acid build-up in your muscles also increases.

The Respiratory System

1) The muscles around your chest get stronger — so they can make your chest cavity larger.

2) With a larger chest cavity, you can breathe more air in — so your vital capacity increases.

3) The bigger your vital capacity, the more oxygen you can take in with one breath. This means the oxygen supply to your muscles will be better — so you'll be able to keep up vigorous exercise for longer.

The Cardiovascular System

1) Your heart is just a muscle — when you exercise it adapts, getting bigger and stronger.

2) A bigger, stronger heart will contract more strongly and pump more blood with each beat — so your stroke volume increase. This means your cardiac output increases too (see p15).

3) The larger your stroke volume, the less often your heart has to beat to pump the same amount of blood around your body. That means your resting heart rate decreases.

4) Physical activity also keeps your blood vessels healthy — your veins and arteries get bigger and stretchier, so your blood pressure falls.

5) The blood vessels also get stronger, so they're less likely to burst under pressure.

Regular Exercise Keeps Your Bones and Joints Healthy

Exercising regularly has great long-term benefits for both your joints and bones:

1) Exercise makes your ligaments and tendons stronger. Just like muscles, your ligaments and tendons adapt when you exercise. Having stronger ligaments and tendons means you're less likely to injure yourself, or develop joint problems like inflammation and osteoarthritis.

2) It increases your bone density. The denser your bones, the stronger they are. The stronger your bones, the less likely they are to break or fracture.

Osteoporosis is a disease where your bone density is so low, your bones are fragile and easily fracture. It often happens in old age when the body is less able to strengthen bone.
You can help prevent osteoporosis by doing weight-bearing exercises (where your legs support your weight) such as walking, running, tennis and aerobics.

Some shocking news — exercise is good for you...

It seems a bit funny at first — to stop your bones becoming weak and easily breakable, make sure you put a large force through them. But it makes sense when you stop and think about it. Remember the best exercises to strengthen your bones are weight-bearing exercises.

Revision Summary — Section Two

Yay... you've made it through the jungle of fancy words and body bits to the end of the section. There's a lot to learn, so as a special revision-based treat I've prepared these lovely questions so you can see how much you've taken in (and how much you've been staring into space or just looking at the pictures). Keep going through them 'til you know all the answers without having to look back at the section. Don't worry if you can't do them all first time round — just keep going through them and it'll click eventually.

1)   Name five functions of the skeleton.

2)   What type of connective tissue joins bones to bones? What's the point of cartilage?

3)   Are muscles attached to bones by: a) ligaments, b) tendons, c) cartilage, or d) sheep?

4)   Draw a picture of: a) a slightly movable joint, and b) a freely movable joint.

5)   Name five types of movement at a joint. (Make sure you can give their proper names as well as describe them.)

6)   Name two types of movable joint. Give two examples of each type of joint.

7)   Say what kinds of movement each type of movable joint will allow. Give an example of an action or activity that relies on that type of joint.

8)   Name the two different types of muscle, and give an example of each type.
     What is the difference between them?

9)   What are the main muscles of the human body? Either label a sketch, or make sure you can name them on your own body. You should be able to name 11 muscle groups.

10) An antagonist relaxes while an agonist does work. **TRUE** or **FALSE**?

11) What's a synergist, and what does it do?

12) Do muscles and joints act as: a) levers, b) pulleys, or c) cranes?

13) What are isotonic and isometric contractions?

14) Draw a rough sketch of the chest cavity, and mark on all the bits of the respiratory system.

15) Where does gaseous exchange take place? What gases are exchanged?

16) Describe aerobic and anaerobic respiration. Give examples of aerobic and anaerobic activities.

17) Why do you still need lots of oxygen after you've finished exercising hard?

18) Explain the term 'vital capacity'.

19) Name the three main functions of the cardiovascular system.

20) What part of your blood carries oxygen around the body?

21) Explain why every blood cell goes through the heart twice on its way round the body.

22) Describe what is meant by a) heart rate, and b) stroke volume.

23) Write down an equation to calculate your cardiac output from your heart rate and stroke volume.

24) What is 'blood pressure'? What are the two readings given when blood pressure is measured?
     Why are they different?

25) What changes 'kick in' when you start to exercise to keep your muscles supplied with oxygen?

26) What substance is responsible for these changes, and what type of substance is it?

27) What does 'blood shunting' mean? How does it help you to stay cool when exercising?

28) List the short-term effects of exercise on a) the muscular system, b) the respiratory system, and c) the cardiovascular system. Now write down the long-term effects on these systems too.

29) Give two ways that the body's recovery from exercise can be speeded up.

30) Describe how exercise can prevent joint and bone problems such as osteoporosis.

Health and Fitness

There are <u>two</u> different kinds of fitness — you need one sort so you can make it up the stairs without passing out, and the other to be good at a particular activity. You need to know about both...

Fitness can be Health-Related or Skill-Related

<u>Fitness</u> means being physically able to meet the <u>demands of your environment</u>.

1) So fitness just means that you're able to do whatever you <u>want</u> or <u>need</u> to do, without getting tired too quickly.

2) There are two basic kinds of fitness — <u>health-related fitness</u> and <u>skill-related fitness</u>.

Trevor definitely felt he was meeting the demands of his environment.

HEALTH-RELATED FITNESS:

This means you're <u>healthy</u>, and can do <u>everyday activities</u> without feeling <u>too tired</u>. It includes:

1) <u>Cardiovascular fitness</u> — your muscles can get enough oxygen to work properly.
2) <u>Muscular strength</u> — you're strong enough to lift, push, pull, etc.
3) <u>Muscular endurance</u> — your muscles don't get tired too quickly.
4) <u>Flexibility</u> — how far you can move different parts of your body.
5) <u>Body composition</u> — you shouldn't be too fat or too thin.

SKILL-RELATED FITNESS:

This is fitness to play a sport at a <u>high level</u>. You need a <u>high level</u> of <u>health-related fitness</u>, as well as some or all of these:

1) <u>Agility</u> — to change direction quickly.
2) <u>Balance</u> — to remain stable.
3) <u>Coordination</u> — to move accurately and smoothly.
4) Fast <u>reactions</u> — to respond quickly.
5) <u>Speed</u>.
6) <u>Power</u> — brute strength combined with speed.

Make sure you know whether each component is health-related or skill-related. More on these components coming up...

You can be Fit Without Being Healthy

1) Health-related <u>fitness</u> is an important part of a <u>healthy, active lifestyle</u>.
2) But you can have a high level of <u>fitness</u> without being <u>physically healthy</u>.

E.g. if your body doesn't get the <u>right nutrients</u> through eating a <u>balanced diet</u>, you won't be <u>healthy</u> — even if you're <u>fit</u> through doing <u>exercise</u>.

<u>Drug</u> use is <u>banned</u> in most sports, but some incredibly fit athletes still use them to improve their performance (see p31). This can have a huge impact on their health.

3) Don't forget — <u>physical</u> health and fitness are only <u>one</u> bit of <u>health</u>. Health also includes your <u>social</u> and <u>mental well-being</u> (see p1). It doesn't matter how physically fit you are — if you're permanently <u>unhappy</u>, you're <u>not</u> healthy.

Phwoar — that bloke's well health-related fit...

So, being fit doesn't mean you're healthy, but it can jolly well help. Make sure you know the <u>definition</u> of 'fitness' — they like to ask multiple choice questions on what key words like <u>fitness</u>, <u>health</u> and <u>exercise</u> mean in the exam. Hang on to your PE kits — there's more fitness fun round the corner...

Endurance and Stamina

<u>Endurance</u> is how long you can do something before you get <u>tired</u>. You need to know about <u>two</u> different types — <u>cardiovascular endurance</u> and <u>muscular endurance</u>. They're both to do with your <u>muscles</u>.

Cardiovascular Endurance <u>Involves your Heart and Lungs</u>

1) Cardiovascular (CV) <u>endurance</u>, cardiovascular <u>fitness</u> and cardiovascular <u>stamina</u> are all different names for the same thing — they're all about keeping your muscles supplied with <u>oxygen</u>.

2) If your <u>heart</u> and <u>lungs</u> can provide a lot of oxygen, your cardiovascular endurance is <u>good</u>. It means you can exercise your <u>whole body</u> without getting too <u>tired</u>.

> <u>CARDIOVASCULAR ENDURANCE/FITNESS/STAMINA</u> is the ability to exercise your <u>whole body</u> for a <u>long</u> time.

3) As your muscles work <u>harder</u>, they need <u>more oxygen</u> — so your <u>breathing</u> and <u>heart rate</u> get faster to move more oxygen around the body.

4) The <u>more efficient</u> your cardiovascular system is, the <u>slower</u> your pulse rate will be (both while resting and exercising), and the <u>quicker</u> it will <u>return to normal</u> after exercise.

5) To <u>improve</u> your cardiovascular endurance, you have to <u>work</u> your <u>heart and lungs</u> hard for <u>at least 15 minutes</u>. This usually means exercising with your heart rate between <u>60%</u> and <u>80%</u> of its maximum (see p42).

Muscular Strength — the Force a Muscle can Exert

1) <u>Muscular strength</u> is just how <u>strong</u> your muscles are (unsurprisingly).

> <u>MUSCULAR STRENGTH</u> is the amount of <u>force</u> that a muscle can apply.

2) Strength is very important in sports where you need to push or pull things using a lot of <u>force</u>, like <u>weightlifting</u> and <u>judo</u>.

3) There are lots of things in <u>everyday life</u> that need strength — like <u>carrying bags of shopping</u> or <u>lifting a small child</u>. Strength is a component of <u>health-related fitness</u> (see p19).

4) If your muscles are strong you're also <u>less</u> likely to <u>injure</u> yourself by picking something up that's <u>heavy</u>.

Muscular Endurance — How Long 'til You get Tired

1) When your voluntary muscles (see p10) have been overworked, they get tired and start to feel <u>heavy</u> or <u>weak</u>.

> <u>MUSCULAR ENDURANCE</u> is the ability to <u>repeatedly</u> use your <u>voluntary</u> muscles <u>over a long time</u>, without getting <u>tired</u>.

2) Muscular endurance is really important in any physical activity where you're using the <u>same muscles repeatedly</u> — e.g. in <u>racquet sports</u> like <u>squash</u> where you have to <u>repeatedly</u> swing your arm.

Dave's muscular endurance was low, his arm felt heavy after 3 swigs of tea.

Your muscles are made up of two different types of fibre. One type (fast twitch fibres) contract very <u>quickly</u> and very <u>powerfully</u> — but they <u>get tired quickly</u>. The second type of fibre (slow twitch fibres) contract more <u>slowly</u> and with <u>less force</u> — but they <u>don't get tired</u> as quickly and so are better for <u>muscular endurance</u>.

The things I have to endure...

Make sure you know the <u>difference</u> between <u>CV</u> and <u>muscular endurance</u> — they're both about your muscles, but CV endurance is about getting <u>oxygen</u> to them, while muscular endurance is how <u>long</u> they can go for.

Flexibility and Body Composition

Flexibility and suppleness are the same thing, and depend on your joints and muscles. They're both about how bendy you are — whether you struggle to touch your toes or you can twist like a pretzel.

Flexibility is your Range of Movement

1) Flexibility is to do with how far your joints move. This depends on the type of joint and the 'stretchiness' of the muscles around it.

> FLEXIBILITY is the amount of movement possible at a joint.

2) It's often forgotten about, but flexibility is dead useful for any physical activity. Here's why...

FEWER INJURIES:

If you're flexible, you're less likely to pull or strain a muscle or stretch too far and injure yourself.

BETTER PERFORMANCE:

You can't do some sports without being flexible — e.g. gymnastics and dance.

Flexibility makes you more efficient in other sports like swimming or hurdling — so you use less energy.

BETTER POSTURE:

More flexibility means a better posture and fewer aches and pains.

Bad posture can lead to permanent deformity of the spine, as well as straining your back.

It can also impair breathing.

Your Body Composition — % of Fat, Muscle and Bone

> BODY COMPOSITION — the percentages of your body weight made up by fat, muscle and bone.

1) If you're healthy, your body will normally be made up of between 15% and 25% body fat.

2) Having too much body fat makes physical activities harder to do.

3) The increased strain on your muscles and joints means you have a higher risk of injuring yourself.

Having a high percentage of body fat often means you have a poor diet, which could lead to other health problems, e.g. heart trouble.

Your BMI is Based on your Height and Weight

1) Your Body Mass Index (BMI) is calculated using your height and weight — you divide your weight (in kg) by your height squared (in metres).

2) It gives you an idea of whether you are underweight, a healthy weight, overweight or obese.

3) However, your BMI doesn't take into account your body composition — athletes like weightlifters will have a high BMI due to the size of their muscles, but it doesn't mean they're actually obese.

BMI	
< 18.5	Underweight
18.5 - 25	Healthy weight
25 - 30	Overweight
> 30	Obese

I like to think my body composition is 20% fat, 80% Hero...

It's important to warm-up before and cool-down after exercise — a good way to do this is by stretching your muscles. It makes you less likely to get injured, and stretching also makes you more flexible. Don't forget to also learn the definition of body composition, what BMI is and why it might be misleading.

Strength, Speed and Power

Strength, speed and power are all different, but they're closely linked.

There are Three Kinds of Strength

There's more to being strong than just being able to lift heavy objects — there are three different kinds of strength. You'll have a mixture of all three.

STATIC STRENGTH

- You use static strength to exert force on a stationary object.
- Your muscles stay the same length, so there's not much movement.
- It's useful in arm-wrestling and a rugby scrum.

EXPLOSIVE STRENGTH

- You use explosive strength to exert force in one very brief, but very fast movement.
- It's closely linked to power (see p23).
- It's useful for the javelin or high jump.

DYNAMIC STRENGTH

- You use dynamic strength to apply force repeatedly over a long time.
- It's linked to endurance.
- It's useful for doing loads of press-ups or cycling.

Most sports need all three kinds of strength — but they're usually not all equally important.

Speed is How Quickly You Move

1) Speed is a measure of how quickly you cover a distance.
2) It can also be how quickly you can carry out a movement, e.g. how quickly you can throw a punch, run a mile or carry out any physical tasks.
3) To work out speed, you just divide the distance covered by the time taken to do it. A fancy way of saying this is 'differential rate'.
4) Speed is important in lots of activities — from the obvious, like a 100 m sprint, to the less obvious, like the speed a hockey player can swing their arm to whack a ball across the pitch.
5) Speed is a component of skill-related fitness, but it can improve your lifestyle too. E.g. being able to do physical jobs quickly means you'll have more leisure time (see p54) to socialise or play sport.

> SPEED is the rate at which someone is able to move, or cover a distance in a given amount of time.

REACTION TIME
This is the time it takes you to respond to something (see next page).

For speed, you need:
1) Fast reaction times,
2) Fast movement times.

MOVEMENT TIME
This is the time it takes you to carry out a certain movement — e.g. a 100 m sprint, or a shot at goal.

You can Increase Your Speed and Reactions By Training

1) You can train to improve your overall speed by improving your cardiovascular endurance. That way you can keep going at speed for longer before getting tired and having to slow down.
2) You can also improve speed by improving the power your muscles can produce (see next page).
3) You can also get quicker by improving your reactions using drills (see p45). E.g. table tennis players can practice rallies whilst standing close to the table so they have less time to react and hit the ball.

I'd rather have super-speed than super-strength...

A man walks towards the corner shop at a speed of 3 miles per hour. The shop is half a mile away. Halfway there, he sees his favourite football player, and sets off running to try to impress him. He runs at a speed of 8 mph. How long will it take him to realise that the shop is shut, and the footballer thinks he is an idiot?

Strength, Speed and Power

So you have the strength, you have the speed, what more could you possibly want? Well, good reactions and ultimate cosmic power would be pretty good too. Reaction time and power are components of skill-related fitness.

Reaction Time is the Time it Takes You to Start Moving

> REACTION TIME is the time it takes you to move in response to something (a 'stimulus').

1) In many sports and activities, you need to have fast reactions to do well.

2) The stimulus you respond to could be a starter gun, a pass in football...

3) You need fast reactions to be able to hit a ball or dodge a punch.
   It doesn't matter how fast you can move, if you don't react in time you'll miss or get hit.

4) Having fast reactions can effectively give you a head start.

Getting away quickly at the start of sprint can be the difference between winning and losing.

Having faster reactions in team sports can help you get away from your opponents, so you can get into better playing positions.

Timing is Important too

1) It's not just your reaction time that matters in sports — your timing is important too.

2) This means things like judging when to pass a ball in football, or when to take off in high jump, or when to overtake in a race.

3) In team games, it's based on your judgements of other people's reaction times — whether it's your team-mates or players from the other team. E.g. if you think you know when someone's going to pass a ball in netball, you can make sure you're there to catch or intercept it.

4) Timing is an example of strategy (a plan of how you're going to win or do well) and decision making — you need to be good at both to do well in sports. E.g. when to push for the finish in a race — too early and you might get overtaken before the end, too late and you might not be able to catch the people in front.

Power Means Speed and Strength Together

Power is a combination of speed and strength. You can develop power by doing plyometrics (see p39).

> POWER is ability to do strength movements quickly.

$$power = strength \times speed$$

Most sports need power for some things — even ones like golf, where it's not obvious.

SPORT	YOU NEED POWER TO...
Football	...shoot
Golf	...drive
Table tennis	...smash
Tennis	...serve and smash
Cricket	...bowl fast and bat

Coordination and balance also help make the most of power — it's not just strength and speed you need.

Strong, powerful, handsome — but enough about me...

Timing is pretty important in everyday life too — get your timing wrong and you'll be late for school, burn your toast or get hit by a flying cow. In those situations, it would be really useful to have the power of time travel. Although 'killed by a flying cow' would be a cool thing to have on your gravestone.

Skill-Related Fitness

There are <u>three</u> more components of <u>skill-related fitness</u> you need to know — agility, balance and coordination. Unless you're doing the OCR courses — which means you can move straight onto the next page.

Agility is Control Over Your Body's Movement

<u>AGILITY</u> is the ability to control the <u>movement</u> of your <u>entire body</u>, and to be able to <u>change</u> your body's <u>position quickly</u>.

Agility is important in any activity where you've got to run about, <u>changing direction</u> all the time, like <u>football</u> or <u>hockey</u>.

Balance is More Than Not Wobbling

Having a good sense of <u>balance</u> means you <u>don't wobble</u> or <u>fall over</u> easily. Great. Unfortunately you have to know a slightly fancier definition of balance for your exam.

BALANCE is the ability to keep your <u>centre of mass</u> over a <u>base support</u>.

1) You can think of the <u>mass</u> of any object as being <u>concentrated</u> at just <u>one point</u>. This point is called the <u>centre of mass</u> (or <u>centre of gravity</u>).

2) If you <u>support</u> an object at its centre of mass (e.g. <u>by hanging</u> it by that point), the object will be perfectly <u>balanced</u>.

3) <u>Everything</u> has a centre of mass — and that includes <u>us</u>.

4) As you change body position, the <u>location</u> of your centre of mass will change too.

5) Whatever activity you're doing, you need to have your centre of mass <u>over</u> whatever is <u>supporting</u> you (your <u>base support</u>) to <u>balance</u>. If you don't, you'll <u>fall over</u>.

This is true whether you're <u>moving</u> (<u>dynamic balance</u>)...

...changing <u>orientation</u> and <u>shape</u> (like in dance and gymnastics)...

...or just staying still (<u>stationary</u> or <u>static balance</u>).

centre of mass

Base support: Geoff

Base support: arms

Base support: legs

Coordination means Using Body Parts Together

<u>COORDINATION</u> is the ability to use <u>two or more</u> parts of your body <u>together</u>.

1) <u>Hand-eye coordination</u> is important in loads of sports. E.g. being able to hit a ball in <u>tennis</u>, or shoot a bullseye in <u>archery</u>.

2) <u>Limb coordination</u> allows you to be able to <u>walk</u>, <u>run</u>, <u>dance</u>...

3) Coordinated movements are smooth and <u>efficient</u>. E.g. a <u>runner</u> with well-coordinated arms and legs will be able to run <u>faster</u> than someone who is less coordinated.

4) Limb coordination is really important in activities like <u>gymnastics</u>, where your performance is judged on your coordination.

Learn your ABC — Agility, Balance and Coordination...

<u>Agility</u>, <u>balance</u> and <u>coordination</u> all go together really. Without being able to coordinate your limbs, you're almost bound to be unbalanced and fall flat on your face. Make sure you know the definitions of each component and what type of activities they're important in.

Age, Gender and Disability

Age, gender and disability can affect a person's performance in most sports. Usually (but not always) men and women have separate competitions — while children don't often compete against adults. You don't need to know this stuff if you're doing the Edexcel or WJEC courses.

Age and Disability can Affect Performance in Sport

AGE

1) STRENGTH — You don't reach your maximum strength until you're fully grown — usually at about 20. In your 20s and 30s, it's still easy to build more muscle. After this, protein levels and muscle mass fall, strength declines and it's harder to build muscle.

2) INJURY & DISEASE — Older people are more likely to injure themselves and it takes longer for them to recover from an injury. Older people generally suffer more from diseases too — cancer and heart disease, for example.

3) FLEXIBILITY — People are most flexible in their teens, so activities like dance and gymnastics are easiest then. After the age of about 30, people generally start to become less flexible.

4) OXYGEN CAPACITY — This falls as you get older — so less oxygen can be taken to the muscles.

5) REACTION TIMES — Your reactions get slower as you get older.

6) EXPERIENCE — Experience is often a vital factor in sport. As you get older, you gain more experience.

BUT — Age doesn't matter for some sports...

If a sport depends on strength or endurance (e.g. weightlifting or marathon running), older people will often be at a disadvantage — but for less strenuous sports (e.g. golf), this doesn't have to be true.

DISABILITY

1) How much a disability affects performance depends on both the disability and the sport — some disabilities will make particular activities harder to do.

2) Many competitions take disability into account by setting up disability categories. That way people with equivalent disabilities can compete against each other, which makes the competition fair.

Gender can Affect Performance too

1) **MEN & WOMEN HAVE DIFFERENT BODIES**
- Men tend to have larger physiques than women.
- They tend to have bigger hearts and lung capacities — which means they often have naturally higher levels of cardiovascular fitness.
- Men's metabolisms are generally better at supplying energy to their muscles, which means they can usually perform better in physical activities than women.

2) **GIRLS MATURE EARLIER THAN BOYS**
- Girls usually reach physical maturity at about 16.
- Boys aren't usually physically mature until about 20.

3) **MEN ARE GENERALLY STRONGER**
Men have bigger muscles, due to higher levels of the hormone testosterone, making them better at activities that rely on strength.

4) **WOMEN ARE GENERALLY MORE FLEXIBLE**
This is partly because they've got less muscle.

Revision should be the main thing on your age-gender...

Make sure you learn how age and gender affect your performance in sport. List the differences between men and women that affect performance, then write down how bodies change with age. There's more on how age and gender can influence the types of sports you choose to do on pages 57 and 58.

Somatotypes

Somatotype means the basic shape of your body. Your somatotype can have a big effect on your suitability for a particular sport. Being the right shape is no guarantee of success, but it helps. If you're doing an OCR or WJEC course, you can just ignore this page and skip onto the next one.

Somatotypes are Body Types

There are three basic somatotypes — ectomorph, mesomorph and endomorph.
Very few people are a perfect example of one of these body types — pretty much everyone is a mixture.
You can think of these basic somatotypes as extremes — at the corners of a triangular graph.

REMEMBER
ENDOMORPH — Dumpy
MESOMORPH — Muscular
ECTOMORPH — Thin

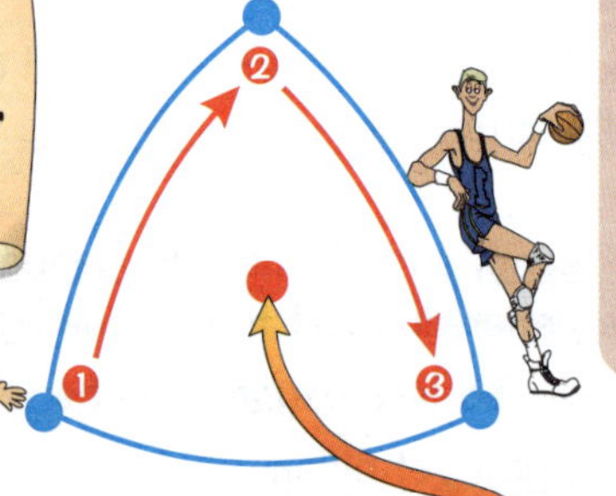

Mr Average would be in the middle of the graph.

② MESOMORPH
1) Wide shoulders and relatively narrow hips.
2) Muscular body.
3) Strong arms and thighs.
4) Not much body fat.

① ENDOMORPH
1) Wide hips but relatively narrow shoulders.
2) A lot of fat on body, arms and legs.
3) Ankles and wrists are relatively slim.

③ ECTOMORPH
1) Narrow shoulders, hips and chest.
2) Not much muscle or fat.
3) Long, thin arms and legs.
4) Thin face and high forehead.

People who play sport at a very high level tend to be closer to the mesomorph corner of the graph, since strength is often important in sport.

Different Somatotypes Suit Different Sports

Sports are usually more suited to certain body types. Having the right body type can give you an advantage.

ECTOMORPHS suit activities like the high jump and long distance running — where being light and tall is an advantage. They don't usually suit activities where strength is important.

E.g. high jumpers need to be light so they have less weight to lift over the bar. The taller the jumper, the smaller the distance they (and their centre of mass) have to travel to be able to get over the bar.

Ideal somatotypes for different sports.

MESOMORPHS are suited to most types of activity.

1) They're able to build up muscle quickly and easily — which gives them an advantage in any activity where strength is important. E.g. sprinting, tennis, weightlifting…
2) Mesomorphs also have broad shoulders, which make it easier for them to be able to support weight using their upper body. This can be a huge advantage in activities like weightlifting and gymnastics.

ENDOMORPHS are usually best at activities like wrestling and shotput — where weight, and a low centre of mass (see p24) can be an advantage.

E.g. in sumo wrestling, being heavy and having a low centre of mass makes it much harder for your opponent to throw you around the wrestling ring.

"This will be the endomorph" — Not a SMart decision…

Be sure to learn the word somatotype. It's a fancy word — but all it means is somebody's shape. Remember — nearly everybody's a mixture of the three basic body types. Learn the names well — it'd be a bad mistake to get the three basic somatotypes confused. Get your learning hat on.

Optimum Weight

Everyone's expected and optimum weight are slightly different, and you need to know why...

Expected and Optimum Weight Depend on Many Things...

1) A person's expected weight is (unsurprisingly) the weight you'd expect them to be, based on their height.

2) Your optimum weight is the weight at which you perform at your best at the activities you do.

3) Two people of the same height are likely to have different optimum weights for many reasons:

   1) BONE STRUCTURE — some people have a larger bone structure than others.
   The more bone you have, the higher your optimum weight will be.

   2) MUSCLE GIRTH — this is a measurement of the circumference (the distance around)
   your muscles when they're flexed. Some people naturally have more muscle than others —
   which means they'll have a larger muscle girth and a higher optimum weight.

   3) GENDER — men and women naturally have different body compositions.
   Men usually have larger bone structures and more muscle than
   women, so men generally have higher optimum weights.

   4) AGE — as you get older you tend to lose muscle and your bone density
   can decrease. So as you age, your optimum weight gets lighter.

   5) ACTIVITY — your optimum weight depends on the activity you want to do.
   A jockey has a low optimum weight, while a heavyweight boxer has a high optimum weight.

Being Underweight or Overweight Affects Performance

Being OVERWEIGHT means weighing more than is normal.

OVERFAT means having more body fat than you should. Being OBESE means being very overfat.

1) Being overweight doesn't necessarily mean you're unhealthy, e.g. you could just have more muscle
than average. Being overweight is usually only harmful when it's caused by being overfat or obese.

2) Being overfat or obese means you're basically carrying extra weight around. It could
be due to a poor diet or over-eating. This can mean you get tired more easily, so
you might not be able to do high endurance sports, e.g. tennis or long distance running.

3) Being overfat or obese can also limit your flexibility and limb movement. The stress the excess
weight puts on the body (especially the heart) can make doing vigorous exercise potentially harmful.

4) Obesity usually has a bad affect on performance, but there are some sports
where you need to be obese to be at your optimum weight (e.g. in sumo wrestling).

5) In sport, you can be classed as underweight if you weigh
less than you need to for your activity.
E.g. being underweight could mean being too light
to fight in a particular weight division.

Being UNDERWEIGHT means weighing less than is normal, needed or healthy.

6) Being underweight because of a poor diet or under-eating may mean you don't have enough
energy or the muscular endurance to do physical activities for long periods of time.

Anorexia is an eating disorder where sufferers believe they're fat and starve themselves to lose weight.
Without sufficient nutrients in their diet, sufferers will feel extremely tired, their muscles will start to
waste away and their bones weaken — doing any physical activity can become extremely difficult.

'Oh Bee City' — a short poem about an insect metropolis...

Now we're getting on to the heavyweight subjects (ho ho ho...). Keep going over this page until you
know what affects someone's optimum weight, and all the underweight and overweight stuff too.

Diet and Nutrition

"You are what you eat," people sometimes say — that's how <u>vital</u> this subject is. It's very important to know about different foods, <u>what</u> they contain, and <u>why</u> we need to eat them.

You Need to Eat a Balanced Diet to be Healthy

1) Eating a balanced diet is an <u>important</u> part of a healthy, active lifestyle.

2) What makes up a balanced diet is slightly <u>different</u> for everyone. E.g. if you exercise loads, you'll need to eat more high energy foods than someone who doesn't.

> A balanced diet contains the <u>best ratio</u> of nutrients to match your lifestyle.

3) If you <u>don't</u> eat a balanced diet, not only could you be <u>physically unable</u> to do the activities you want to, but you might actually be <u>damaging</u> your body, e.g. if you eat a lot of <u>fatty foods</u>, you might end up with <u>high blood pressure</u>, which increases the risk of <u>heart disease</u> and <u>strokes</u>.

You Need More of Some Nutrients Than Others

There are <u>two</u> main groups of nutrients your body needs:

<u>Macro nutrients</u> — nutrients your body needs in <u>large</u> amounts.

<u>Micro nutrients</u> — nutrients your body still needs, but in <u>smaller</u> amounts.

MACRO NUTRIENTS:
1) Proteins
2) Carbohydrates
3) Fats

MICRO NUTRIENTS:
1) Vitamins
2) Minerals

WATER AND DIETARY FIBRE

On top of these, you also need plenty of <u>water</u> and <u>dietary fibre</u> in your diet to be healthy. The best way to get all of these nutrients is to eat a <u>varied</u> diet with plenty of <u>fruit</u> and <u>vegetables</u>, but not too much <u>fat</u>.

Carbohydrates, Fats and Proteins are Macro Nutrients

Carbohydrates, fats and proteins are <u>macro nutrients</u> — they make up the bulk of your food. They provide you with <u>energy</u> and help you <u>grow</u>.

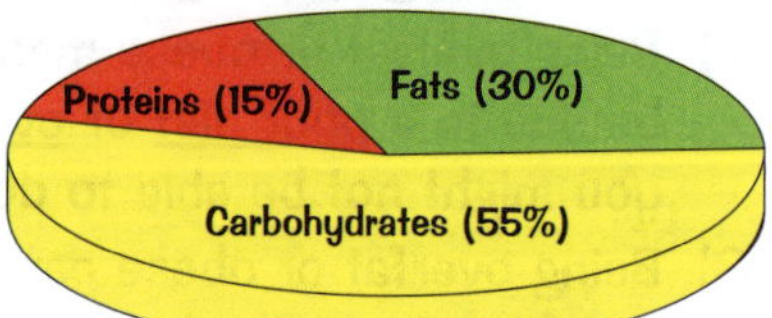

CARBOHYDRATES

1) Carbohydrates are the main source of <u>energy</u> for the body.

2) You can get <u>simple</u> ones e.g. sugar, and <u>complex</u> ones e.g. starch.

3) Whenever you eat carbohydrates, some will get <u>used</u> by the body <u>straight away</u>.

4) The rest gets <u>stored</u> in the liver and muscles ready for when it's needed.

PROTEINS

1) Proteins help the body <u>grow</u> and <u>repair itself</u>.

2) They're made from molecules called <u>amino acids</u> — your body can make most amino acids but some you have to get from food.

This pie chart (mmm, pie) shows about how much of each nutrient you should eat.

FATS

1) Fats are made from molecules called <u>fatty acids</u> and <u>glycerol</u>.

2) They provide <u>energy</u> for the body but they're also really important for helping keep the <u>body warm</u> and <u>protecting organs</u>. There are also some <u>vitamins</u> that the body can <u>only</u> absorb using fats.

3) Some fats are turned into <u>cholesterol</u> by the <u>liver</u>. Cholesterol can be transported in <u>high</u> or <u>low density lipoproteins</u> (<u>HDLs</u> and <u>LDLs</u>). Having <u>too much LDL</u> cholesterol increases the risk of <u>heart attacks</u> and <u>strokes</u>. Having high levels of <u>HDLs</u> is <u>good</u>, as it helps the body get rid of excess cholesterol.

If you are what you eat, would French fries turn you French?

Energy value is measured in <u>kilojoules</u> (<u>kJ</u>) or <u>kilocalories</u> (<u>kcal</u>) — but people usually say <u>calories</u> instead of kilocalories. Anyway, this page might look pretty full, but really it's just a <u>definition</u>, <u>three blue boxes</u> and a <u>pie</u> made from 15% protein, 30% fat and 55% sweet, sweet, sugar... err I mean carbohydrate.

Diet and Nutrition

Micro nutrients are just as important as macro nutrients — you just need smaller amounts of them.

You need Small Amounts of Vitamins and Minerals

VITAMINS

1) Vitamins help keep your bones, teeth and skin healthy.
2) They're also needed for many of the body's chemical reactions.

> With a properly balanced diet, you don't need vitamin supplements.

FAT-SOLUBLE VITAMINS — can be stored in the body.

E.g. Vitamin A — needed for your growth and vision, and can be found in vegetables, eggs and liver.

Vitamin D — needed for strong bones, so you don't get bone-softening diseases like osteoporosis (see p17). Vitamin D can be made by the skin in sunshine, but it's also found in milk, fish, liver and eggs.

WATER-SOLUBLE VITAMINS — can't be stored, so you need to eat them regularly.

E.g. Vitamin C — good for your skin and the stuff that holds your body tissues together. Without it, your body tissues can't form properly and you get a nasty disease called scurvy. Vitamin C is found in fruit and veg — especially citrus fruits like oranges and lemons.

Earl   Mini-earl

MINERALS

1) These are needed for healthy bones and teeth, and to build other tissues.
2) Minerals help in various chemical reactions in the body.

E.g. Calcium is needed for strong bones and teeth, and also for muscle contractions (see p11). There's lots in green vegetables, milk, cheese and some fish.

Iron is handy for making red blood cells (see p8). Without it your blood can't carry much oxygen. There's tons in liver, beans and green vegetables.

Water and Dietary Fibre are Just as Important

WATER

1) Water's needed in loads of chemical reactions in the body. It's also lost in your breath, sweat, urine and faeces.
2) If you don't drink enough to replace what your body uses or loses you'll become dehydrated, and you won't perform as well.
3) If you drink more than you need, your kidneys will produce more urine to get rid of the excess.

DIETARY FIBRE

1) You need fibre to keep your digestive system working properly.
2) There's lots of fibre in fruit and vegetables — another good reason to eat loads of them.

Not the best way to increase your fibre intake

Your Diet can help Improve your Performance

1) Most athletes plan their diets to help improve their performance — e.g. runners will eat lots of carbohydrates before an event, while weightlifters eat lots of protein to build up their muscles.

2) When you eat is also important — you should eat lots of carbohydrates before exercising, but don't eat anything immediately before, during or immediately after exercising (you should drink lots of water though).

3) Thanks to blood shunting (see p15) your digestive system has a limited blood supply when you exercise. Any food in your digestive system won't be able to be digested properly, so you're more likely to feel sick.

A balanced diet — a pie in each hand...

There's lots of fun stuff to learn on this page. Each point's a doddle by itself, so just take it a bit at a time — soon you'll be reeling those facts off faster than a puppy can pull on toilet paper...

Recreational Drugs

Recreational drugs (i.e. drugs people take for enjoyment) can have a negative effect on your health and can affect your performance in sports. If you're doing the WJEC or AQA courses you can just skip this page.

Alcohol Damages your Performance

Although alcohol is legal, it's still a drug and can affect your performance badly.

1) It affects your coordination, speech and judgement, so you're more likely to hurt yourself. You're also less likely to be able to do things accurately — like shoot in football or return the ball in tennis.

2) It slows your reactions, whether it's to a starter gun in a race or a pass in netball.

3) It makes your muscles get tired more quickly, so you can't exercise for as long.

4) It increases your blood pressure — the more you drink, the higher it gets.

5) Eventually it damages your liver, kidneys, heart, muscles, brain, and the digestive and immune systems.

Small amounts of alcohol don't do too much harm, but drinking before you do sports can be dangerous — you're more likely to have an accident or hurt others. If you want to have a healthy, active lifestyle and do well in sports, it's best to only drink in moderation (or not at all).

Tobacco is Legal but Harmful

Tobacco is another legal drug, but it's really bad for you.
Every cigarette damages your body and affects your performance in sports.

1) Smoking causes nose, throat and chest irritations.

2) It makes you short of breath, so you find it harder to exercise.

3) Smoking and nicotine cause a temporary rise in blood pressure.

4) It damages your respiratory system (see below) and your cardiovascular system (see p12-14). Smoking increases the risk of developing heart disease, cancer, bronchitis, and other diseases.

For a healthy, active life it's best to avoid smoking altogether.

Smoking Clogs Up the Alveoli

1) Smoking has a really bad effect on your respiratory system.

2) Cigarette smoke contains tar, which clogs up the alveoli and makes it harder for gas exchange to take place. Eventually the alveoli will collapse and stop working.

3) Even if the tar is removed and the alveoli are repaired, they'll never be as efficient as they were.

4) Cigarette smoke also contains the addictive drug and poison nicotine. Nicotine causes the blood vessels in the lungs to tighten, which slows the blood flow in the lungs making the gas exchange in the alveoli less efficient.

Doesn't sound like fun to me...

Some people use alcohol and tobacco to calm their nerves and improve their performance — some darts players drink alcohol whilst they play to help get them 'in the zone'. But, alcohol affects your judgement, coordination and reactions — so it usually has a negative effect your performance.

Performance-Enhancing Drugs

Some people cheat by taking drugs. Drugs can sometimes make them perform better, but there are risks...
If you're doing an AQA course, you don't need to know these bits.

Many Drugs can Improve Performance

Some athletes use drugs to improve their performance. The use of these drugs
in sport is usually banned, and they usually have nasty side effects.
Unfortunately, some athletes still break the rules by taking them anyway —
even with the risks. (Breaking the rules like this is sometimes called deviance.)
These are the drugs you need to know about:

REMEMBER — BAD SNaP

B — Beta blockers
A — Anabolic steroids
D — Diuretics
S — Stimulants
Na — Narcotic analgesics
P — Peptide hormones

BETA BLOCKERS

- Are drugs that control heart rate.
- They lower the heart rate, steady shaking hands, and have a calming, relaxing effect.

But...

- They can cause low blood pressure, cramp and heart failure.

STIMULANTS

- Affect the central nervous system (the bits of your brain and spine that control your reactions).
- They can increase mental and physical alertness.

But...

- They can lead to high blood pressure, heart and liver problems, and strokes.
- They're addictive.

ANABOLIC STEROIDS

- Mimic the male sex hormone testosterone.
- Testosterone increases your bone and muscle growth (so you can get bigger and stronger). It can also make your more aggressive.

But...

- They cause high blood pressure, heart disease, infertility and cancer.
- Women may grow facial and body hair, and their voice may deepen.

NARCOTIC ANALGESICS

- Kill pain — so injuries and fatigue don't affect performance so much.

But...

- They're addictive, with unpleasant withdrawal symptoms.
- Feeling less pain can make an athlete train too hard.
- They can lead to constipation and low blood pressure.

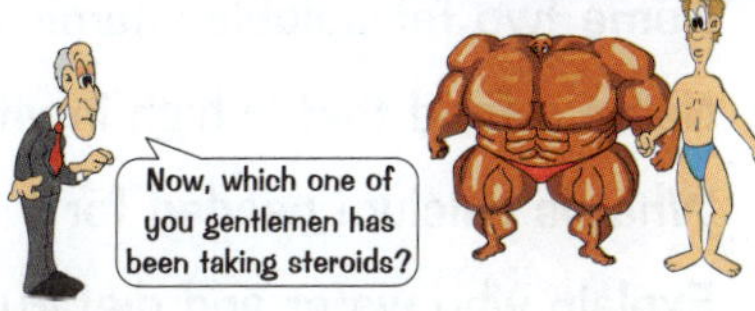

DIURETICS

- Increase the amount you urinate, causing weight loss — important if you're competing in a certain weight division.
- Can mask traces of other drugs in the body.

But...

- They can cause cramp and dehydration.

PEPTIDE HORMONES

- Cause the production of other hormones — similar to anabolic steroids.
- EPO (Erythropoietin) is a peptide hormone that causes the body to produce more red blood cells.

But...

- They can cause strokes and abnormal growth.

Blood Doping is Banned

You can improve your performance by increasing the number of red blood cells in your bloodstream to
increase the oxygen supply to your muscles.

You can do this by altitude training (see p40) or cheat and get the same effect by blood doping.

Blood doping can be done in different ways.

1) Before a competition an athlete can be injected with red blood cells.
   Possible side effects of injecting red blood cells include allergic reactions, kidney damage
   and blocked capillaries or, if the blood is from someone else, catching viruses such as HIV.

2) Athletes can also take EPO to increase their red blood cell count (see peptide hormones above).

Anna Bolic — don't mess with her...

Athletes have to give blood and urine samples to be tested for drugs. Testing can happen at any time, and
refusing to give a sample can be just as bad as failing a drug test. Punishments for failing a drug test can
include lifetime bans from the sport — that's not to mention all the damage the drugs do to their bodies.

Revision Summary — Section Three

I bet all that talk of diet, nutrition and pie (mmm, pie) has made you hungry. Well, you can nip off and make yourself a nice (healthy) snack, just as soon as you've answered a few questions on this section. Get ready for a whirlwind tour of the joys of health, fitness and pie.

1) Name the three types of macro nutrient. Name the two types of micro nutrient.

2) As well as macro and micro nutrients, what two other things do you need for a balanced diet?

3) About what percentage of protein should you have in your diet?

4) Name two fat-soluble vitamins.

5) Name a food that is high in vitamin C.

6) What is calcium needed for?

7) Explain why water and dietary fibre are important in a balanced diet.

8) Is cardiovascular fitness a part of health-related fitness or skill-related fitness?

9) Which two organs are involved in cardiovascular fitness?

10) Describe fast twitch and slow twitch fibres.

11) Define 'flexibility'.

12) Name the three things that make up your body composition.

13) Name and describe the three kinds of strength.

14) Define 'speed'.

15) What is reaction time?

16) Describe 'power'.

17) What do the letters stand for in the ABC of skill-related fitness?

18) Give four ways age could affect your performance in sport.

19) Give three ways gender could affect your performance in sport.

20) Name the three somatotypes and write down their main characteristics.

21) For each somatotype, write down one sport it's suited to.

22) Name three factors that affect your optimum weight.

23) Describe what the terms 'underweight' and 'overweight' mean.

24) What is obesity? What is anorexia?

25) Name two recreational drugs and explain what effects they can have.

26) What do beta blockers do?

27) What are the side effects of stimulants?

28) Name two other performance-enhancing drugs.

29) Describe blood doping.

30) Name three possible side effects of blood doping.

PAR-Q and Personal Readiness

If you want to try a new physical activity, make sure it's appropriate — fill in a PAR-Q and have some health checks to make sure you're fit enough to do it. Otherwise you might do yourself more harm than good.

Choose an Activity That's Appropriate for You

It's important to choose and activity that you're fit enough to start and is suitable for you. What you choose might depend on a few things:

FITNESS LEVELS —
You should start at a level that's right for you. It's probably not a good idea to try and run a marathon if you're only used to walking down the shops.

PHYSICAL MATURITY —
Someone who's still growing might not have the strength or endurance for high intensity sports, and could permanently injure themselves by doing them.

AGE —
As you get older your body becomes weaker, so older people might prefer non-contact sports instead of sports like rugby or boxing, where it's more likely they will get injured.

PAR-Q — Physical Activity Readiness Questionnaire

Once you've decided on an activity, you need to make sure you're physically ready and able to do it.

1) Increasing the amount of physical activity you do is normally a safe thing to do — but if you have an injury or physical problem it could damage your health.

2) PAR-Qs are questionnaires made up of 'yes or no' questions, designed to assess your personal readiness (whether it's safe for you) to increase your physical activity.

3) If you answer no to all of the questions, you can be fairly sure it's safe for you to increase your physical activity.

4) If you answer yes to any of the questions, you need to visit your doctor to make sure it's safe first.

PAR-Q	Yes	No
1) Have you ever experienced any chest pain while doing physical activity?	☐	☐
2) Have you ever been diagnosed with a heart problem?	☐	☐
3) Are you currently being prescribed any medication?	☐	☐
4) Do you have a joint problem that may be made worse by physical activity?	☐	☐

Health Screening Makes Sure You're in Tip Top Condition

Health screening is another way to assess your personal readiness before you start an activity. Here are the health checks and tests you need to know:

MEASURING BLOOD PRESSURE
Exercise can put a lot of stress on the body. High or low blood pressure could indicate a problem with your heart or cardiovascular system (see p14) — which could make it dangerous to start doing vigorous exercise.

CHECKING LIFESTYLE AND FAMILY HISTORY
Looking at your lifestyle and checking your family medical history might give clues about any health problems you might suffer. You're more likely to suffer from some things if your parents or grandparents had them, e.g. high blood pressure or heart disease.

MEASURING BODY MASS INDEX (BMI)
BMI is a way of working out if you're at a healthy weight (see p21). But, it only takes into account your height and not your age or fitness.

MEASURING RESTING HEART RATE
Resting heart rate is a good measure of cardiovascular fitness. The lower your resting heart rate, the better your cardiovascular system is (see p14).

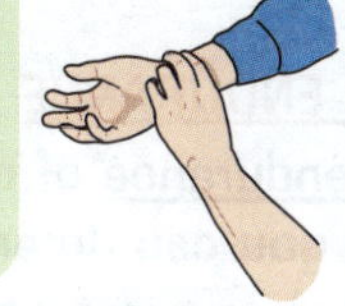

NB: a resting heart rate of 0 bpm doesn't mean you're hyper fit...

With all tests, you should check:

1) its validity — does it test what it should?
2) its reliability — does it give repeatable, consistent results?

E.g. BMI is a very reliable test — it'll give you exactly the same result for the same height and weight each time. It might not be a very valid test for everyone though, e.g. being healthy but having a lot of muscle could give a BMI indicating an unhealthy weight.

Want to go extreme shopping? — Let's PAR-Q and Ride...

Being fit is really important, but there's no point trying to improve your fitness if you're just going to do yourself a mischief. By filling out a PAR-Q and testing fitness before you start, you lower your chances of getting injured. Make sure you know the health screening tests and why they're important too.

Fitness Testing

You should to <u>test</u> your fitness <u>before</u> and <u>during</u> your training so you can see if you're improving.

You Need to Know Tests for Cardiovascular Endurance...

COOPER'S 12-MINUTE RUN TEST

1) <u>Jog</u> to warm up.
2) Then <u>run</u> around a track as many times as you can in 12 minutes.
3) The further you can run, the fitter you are.

TREADMILL TEST

1) Treadmill tests usually test <u>how long</u> you can run for.
2) Start walking with the treadmill on a slow/flat setting, then gradually increase the <u>slope</u> and/or the <u>speed</u>.
3) The <u>longer</u> you can run for, the <u>fitter</u> you are.

MULTI-STAGE FITNESS TEST (MSFT)

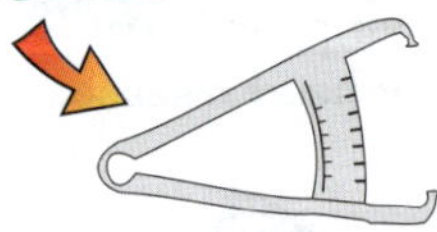

1) A recording of a series of <u>timed bleeps</u> is played.
2) You have to run 'shuttles' between 2 lines, 20 metres apart, starting on the first bleep.
3) Your foot must be <u>on</u> or <u>over</u> the next line when the next bleep sounds.
4) After about a minute the time between bleeps gets <u>shorter</u>, so you have to <u>run</u> faster.
5) If you miss a bleep you are allowed two further bleeps to catch up. If you miss <u>three</u> bleeps in a row, the <u>level</u> and <u>number</u> of shuttles completed are noted as your final score.

HARVARD STEP TEST

1) Using a 45 cm step, do <u>30 step-ups a minute</u> for 5 minutes. (Or if you have to go slower, keep going for <u>20 seconds</u> after you <u>begin</u> to slow down, then stop.)
2) <u>Rest</u> for 1 minute, then take your pulse for 15 seconds — multiply this by 4 to get your heart rate.
3) Use this <u>formula</u> to work out your score — the higher your score, the fitter you are.

$$\frac{\text{length of exercise in seconds} \times 100}{5.5 \times \text{pulse count}}$$

4) There are different versions of the Harvard step test so check the details (height of the step, rest time etc.) before comparing results.

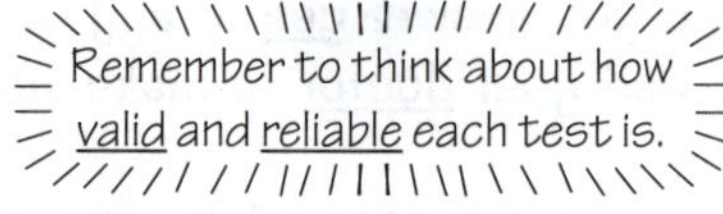

Remember to think about how <u>valid</u> and <u>reliable</u> each test is.

...And Other Components of Health-Related Fitness Too

BODY COMPOSITION — CALLIPERS AND BODY DENSITY TEST

1) <u>Skin fold callipers</u> are used to pinch your <u>skin</u> and <u>underlying fat</u> — you can plug these measurements into an equation to estimate your <u>body fat percentage</u>. To get a good estimate, you have to be pinched in the <u>right way</u>. The percentage of your total body fat stored under the skin depends on factors like <u>age</u> and <u>gender</u>. You can use <u>different equations</u> to take this into account and make your estimate more <u>accurate</u>.

2) In a <u>body density test</u>, you weigh yourself on <u>land</u> and <u>underwater</u>. Then, you can use the two measurements and some clever maths, to work out your body density and <u>percentage body fat</u>.

MUSCULAR ENDURANCE — SIT-UPS AND PRESS-UPS

To test the <u>endurance</u> of different muscles, see <u>how many times</u> you can do an exercise — e.g. abdominal curls (sit-ups) or press-ups.

MUSCULAR STRENGTH — HAND GRIP TEST

This kind of <u>dynamometer</u> measures <u>hand</u> and <u>forearm strength</u>. Just grip as hard as you can...

FLEXIBILITY — SIT AND REACH TEST

This measures <u>flexibility</u> in the <u>back</u> and <u>lower hamstrings</u>.

1) Sit on the floor with your legs pointing <u>straight</u> out in front of you.
2) Push a ruler, placed on a box, as far <u>forwards</u> as you can with your fingers — keeping your legs <u>straight</u> all the time.

Yikes — that's a lorra lorra testing...

This page is choca-block... mmmmm chocolate... sorry... must focus. There's lots of ways to <u>test</u> your <u>health-related fitness</u> and I'm afraid there's no way round it — you've just got to sit and learn 'em.

Fitness Testing

You've got to know how to test all these components of <u>skill-related fitness</u> too. Here's the info...

You can Test Your Agility, Balance and Coordination...

AGILITY — ILLINOIS AGILITY RUN TEST

1) Set out a course using cones like this:
2) Start <u>lying face down</u> at the start cone. When a start whistle blows, run around the circuit as fast as you can.
3) The course is set up so you have to constantly <u>change direction</u>.
4) The <u>more agile</u> you are, the <u>quicker</u> you'll be able to complete the course.

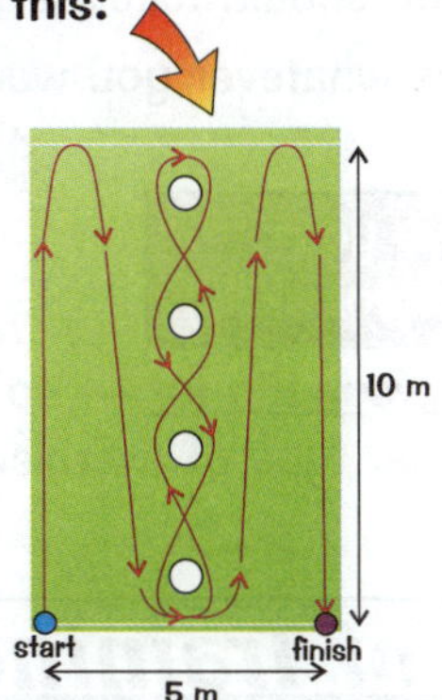

COORDINATION — 3-BALL JUGGLE

To be able to juggle, you need to be <u>coordinated</u>. The better your coordination, the <u>longer</u> you should be able to juggle for.

BALANCE — THE STANDING STORK TEST

Stand on your best leg on your tip toes with your other foot touching your knee and your hands on your hips. Time how long you can stand there. <u>Wobbling</u>'s allowed, but no moving your feet or hands. Take the <u>best of three</u> times.

COORDINATION — ALTERNATE HAND THROW

1) For this you need to stand in front of a <u>wall</u>.
2) <u>Throw</u> a ball from your <u>right</u> hand against a wall and <u>catch</u> it in your <u>left</u> — then throw it from your left hand back against the wall and catch it in your right.
3) The <u>more</u> throws and catches you can do in 30 seconds, the <u>better</u> your <u>coordination</u>.

...as well as Your Speed, Reactions and Power

REACTIONS — THE RULER DROP TEST

1) Get a friend to hold a ruler <u>vertically</u> between your thumb and first finger. The <u>0 cm</u> mark on the ruler should be <u>in line</u> with the <u>top of your thumb</u>.
2) Your friend drops the ruler — you have to try and catch it <u>as soon as you see it drop</u>.
3) Read off the distance the ruler fell before you managed to catch it. The <u>slower</u> your reactions, the longer it takes you to catch the ruler, so the further up the ruler you'll catch it.

POWER — STANDING BROAD JUMP TEST

This is just like doing the long jump, but from a <u>standing start</u>.

1) Stand behind a line with both your feet next to each other.
2) <u>Jump</u> as far <u>forward</u> as you can (you can swing your arms to help you jump further), <u>landing on both feet</u>.
3) How far you jump depends on the <u>power</u> your leg muscles can produce. The greater the power, the further you jump.

POWER — SARGENT/VERTICAL JUMP TEST

1) Put chalk on your finger tips and stand <u>side-on</u> to a wall.
2) Raise the arm that's nearest the wall and mark the <u>highest point</u> you can reach.
3) Still standing side-on to the wall, <u>jump</u> and <u>mark the wall</u> as high up as you can.
4) The more <u>powerful</u> your leg muscles are, the larger the <u>distance between</u> your first mark and second mark.

SPEED —
30 M/50 M SPRINT TEST

Simply time how long it takes you to <u>run 30</u> or <u>50 m</u>.

There are Also Some Simple Ways to Monitor Fitness

DIARY KEEPING — this is an easy way of <u>recording</u> the amount of activity you do. It's good for <u>monitoring improvements</u> in your fitness.

PEDOMETERS — these record the <u>number of steps</u> you take. They can be used to work out how many calories you've burnt.

HEART RATE MONITORS — these (unsurprisingly) <u>monitor</u> your <u>heart rate</u>. You can see how <u>strenuous</u> an activity is by measuring how much your heart rate goes <u>up</u>.

Learn this page — and give your brain a stretch...

Just like you get tested on how much you know about PE, athletes get tested on things like <u>muscle strength</u>, <u>endurance</u> and <u>flexibility</u> — so you've got to know how to test them too. Get scribbling...

Training Sessions

Training's not about running for as long as possible, or lifting the heaviest weights you can.
There's much more to it than that — and you'll be asked about it in the exam, so get reading.

Train to Improve Your Health, Fitness or Performance

1) To improve your health, fitness or performance, you should follow a Personal Exercise Programme (PEP).

2) A PEP is a training programme designed to improve whatever you want it to improve — it could be your general health and fitness, or a particular skill.

> TRAINING — a programme designed to improve your performance, physical fitness, or skills (including motor skills).

> A motor skill is a learned set of movements that make up a smooth, efficient action e.g. walking, or a tennis serve.

3) A PEP needs to be interesting and must suit the person it's for — so you've got to find out about them. Which means asking them some questions like: What type of exercise do you like? How fit are you now? There's more about creating a PEP on page 41.

SPORT — The Five Principles of Training

To get the most from your training you should follow the principles of SPORT.

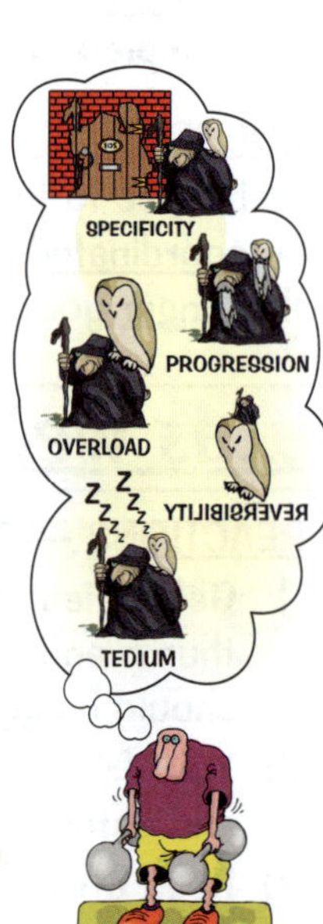

S → SPECIFICITY / INDIVIDUAL NEEDS — Every person will need a different training programme suited to them and the sport they want to do.

1) Train the parts of the body that are specific to that sport — there's no point making a weightlifter run 10 miles a day — it won't improve their weightlifting.
2) Training needs to be done at the right level for the individual — if someone's dead unfit, don't start them with a 5-mile swim.

P → PROGRESSION — Steadily increase the amount of training that's done.

But only when the body has adapted to the previous training, so you avoid injury.

O → OVERLOAD — You've got to make your body work harder than it normally would.

Overload is the only way to get fitter. You can overload by increasing the frequency, intensity, or the duration of the training (see next page).

R → REVERSIBILITY — any fitness improvement or body adaptation caused by training will gradually reverse and be lost when you stop training.

It takes much longer to gain fitness than to lose fitness, which isn't ideal.

> The 'R' stands for 'rest and recovery' in the Edexcel courses.

T → TEDIUM — The time you spend training needs to be interesting as well as useful.

You need to do different things in each session — otherwise you'll get bored and never want to do any training at all.

You Need to Rest and Recover After Training

1) You also need to allow time for your body to repair itself and recover after vigorous exercise.

> REST and RECOVERY: Recovery is the time needed for your body to repair any damage caused by physical activity. Rest is the amount of time you allow your body to recover.

2) You need to rest until your body has fully recovered, or you'll just end up injuring yourself.
3) But, if you rest for too long, reversibility will mean you'll lose all the benefits of doing the training.
4) If you get injured, not only have you got to wait for your injury to heal, but, thanks to reversibility, your fitness will start to decrease while you do.

S, P, O, R, T — what a convenient set of letters...

SPORT — it's a nice way to remember the principles of training but don't forget about rest and recovery too — you could think SPORRT to help you remember, which has the added bonus of sounding more piratey.

Training Sessions

The best training programmes aren't just thrown together — they have to be carefully planned.

Training Programmes can be Planned using FITT

Frequency, intensity and time are all part of making sure you overload while you're training.

F = FREQUENCY of activity — how often you should exercise.

E.g. if you just want to stay healthy you should exercise for at least 20 minutes three to five times a week. If you do a hard workout you should give your body at least 24 hours rest before you exercise again.

I = INTENSITY of activity — how hard you should exercise.

E.g. if you wanted to lose weight you should raise your heart rate to about 75% of your maximum safe heart rate for 20 minutes or more (see p42).

T = TIME spent on activity — how long you should exercise.

Training sessions to improve cardiovascular fitness tend to last for 20 minutes or longer. Strength training sessions are generally shorter and less sustained.

T = TYPE of activity — what exercises you should use.

It can be good to vary training sessions to stop you tiring and getting bored of the same old workout. In aerobic training this is called cross-training — a different exercise (e.g. cycling instead of running) is used to increase fitness, but without over-stressing the tissues and joints used in your main activity.

Eventually your body will adapt to the training — you'll get fitter, and your performance and competence will improve. All training programmes need to be constantly monitored to make sure that the activities are still producing overload. As you get fitter your PEP will need to change to keep improving your fitness.

Always Warm-Up First and Cool-Down Afterwards

All exercise and training sessions should be made up of a warm-up, a main activity, and a cool-down.

WARM-UP
Gets your body ready for exercise.
1) Increases blood flow to the muscles — so they can do the work later on in the training.
2) Stretches the muscles, moves the joints and increases flexibility — so you're ready for the work and less likely to injure yourself.
3) Helps to improve the strength and speed of muscle contractions.
4) Concentrates the mind on the training.

COOL-DOWN
Gets your body back to normal.
1) Helps replace the oxygen in your muscles, and so gets rid of any lactic acid and other waste products.
2) Helps prevent injuries and soreness the following day.

A Training Plan Should Suit the Activity

1) Your training should match the type of activity or component of fitness you want to improve.
2) If you want to be good at an aerobic activity like long distance running — you should do a lot of aerobic activity as part of your training.
3) For anaerobic activities like sprinting, you need to do anaerobic training so your muscles are able to cope with the lactic acid build up and get better at getting rid of it.
4) Lots of activities are a mixture of aerobic and anaerobic activity, so a training plan for these sorts of activities will have a bit of both types of training in it.

Make sure you can FITT everything in your training plan...

Use FITT to get fit — Frequency, Intensity, Time and Type. Remember you need to warm-up before and cool-down after exercise and your training has to suit the activity — like cheese has to suit the cracker...

Training Methods

So, training should make you better at whatever it is you're training for. For this to work, you need to match the type of training with what you want to do. There are nine main training methods you need to know.

1) Weight Training Improves Muscular Strength

When you weight train, you contract your muscles.
There are two ways to do weight training — each type uses a different kind of muscle contraction.

1) You can train by increasing the tension in a muscle, without changing the muscle's length (so there's no movement). You can do this by pressing against stationary objects.

EXAMPLE: THE WALL SIT
Sit with your back to the wall and your knees bent at 90° and hold it.

2) You can also train by contracting your muscles to make your limbs move.

3) Each completed movement is called a 'rep' (repetition), and you've got to finish a 'set' (group of reps) before a rest.

EXAMPLE: PULL-UPS
Hang from a bar and then pull yourself up until your head is over it.

4) Both types of weight training can be used to develop muscular strength and muscular endurance.

5) For the training to improve your fitness, you need to overload (see p37).

6) Weight training is a type of anaerobic training. It's good for improving performance in anaerobic activities such as sprinting. It can also just be a great way to improve your health-related fitness.

OVERLOAD is achieved by lifting the weights more times (increasing the reps or sets), or using heavier weights.

2) Continuous Training Means No Resting

1) Continuous training involves exercising at a constant rate doing activities like running or cycling.

2) It usually means exercising so that your heart rate is between 60% and 80% of its maximum.

3) Of course, you need to overload during training to get fitter.

4) As well as improving your cardiovascular fitness and muscular endurance, it's also good for using up body fat and improving your body composition.

5) Continuous training is only made up of aerobic activity — so it's good training for activities like marathon running.

OVERLOAD is achieved by increasing the duration, distance, speed, or frequency of the training.

3) Fartlek Training is all about Changes of Speed

1) Fartlek training can be made easy or hard to suit your fitness and can be adapted to fit any continuous exercise (e.g. running, cycling, swimming, rowing).

2) It involves changes in intensity and type of exercise without stopping.

For example, part of a fartlek run could be to sprint for 10 seconds, then jog for 20 seconds (repeated for 4 minutes) — followed by long-stride running for 2 minutes.

OVERLOAD is achieved by increasing the times or speeds of each bit, or the terrain difficulty (e.g. running uphill).

3) It's a mix of aerobic and anaerobic activity, so it's good training for activities that need different paces, like football and basketball.

4) The really good thing about fartlek training is that it can be easily changed to suit an individual or activity.

Nige's fartlek training:
Run for 1 minute
Bathe for 30 minutes

Fartlek training .... (Add your own joke.)

So you want muscles like Arnie...? Well, this is the topic that'll tell you how to do it — kind of.
But never mind what you want, the examiners will want you to be able to churn out all the major points that are mentioned on these few pages. You know the drill — cover up the page and get scribbling...

Training Methods

Circuit and cross training are great for increasing <u>endurance</u> — and plyometric training makes you... explosive.

4) Circuit Training Uses Loads of Different Exercises

1) Each circuit has between 6 and 10 <u>stations</u> in it. At each station you do a <u>specific exercise</u> for a <u>set amount of time</u> before moving onto the next station. You're allowed a <u>short rest</u> between stations.

2) All the exercises are <u>different</u>, which makes circuit training a lot more <u>interesting</u> than some other training methods.

3) Circuit training can be <u>easily adapted</u> to suit you.

OVERLOAD is achieved by doing <u>more repetitions</u> at each station, completing the circuit <u>more quickly</u>, <u>resting less</u> between stations, or by repeating the circuit.

A circuit's 'stations' might include <u>weight training</u>, or <u>aerobic</u> exercises...
Because you <u>design</u> the circuit, you can use circuit training to improve <u>muscular endurance</u>, <u>strength</u>, <u>cardiovascular fitness</u>... anything you want really.

5) Cross Training Improves Overall Performance

1) <u>No single exercise</u> will improve <u>all</u> components of health-related and skill-related fitness <u>equally well</u>.

2) By picking activities that use different <u>muscle groups</u> or focus on different components of fitness, you can improve your <u>general overall fitness</u> — this is <u>cross training</u>.

3) In cross training, you can do activities that focus on one muscle group while waiting for another set of muscles to recover. This means you can <u>train more</u>, but without the risk of getting <u>injured</u>.

4) Because you're doing different activities, it can be a lot more <u>interesting</u> than some of the other training methods.

5) Whatever activities you do as part of cross training, you still need to <u>overload</u> to improve your fitness.

6) As with circuit training, you can <u>adapt</u> cross training to improve whichever skill or component of fitness you want to.

EXAMPLE: A swimmer might decide to take up <u>squash</u> and <u>cycling</u>. These activities still help improve <u>cardiovascular fitness</u> but use different muscles to swimming.

6) Plyometric Training Improves Power

For lots of sports it's important to have <u>explosive strength</u> and <u>power</u> e.g. for fast starts in sprinting (see p22-23). You can train muscular power using <u>plyometrics</u>.

1) When muscles contract, they can either <u>shorten</u> or <u>lengthen</u>, e.g. during a bicep curl.

- During the upward movement of a bicep curl the muscle <u>contracts</u> and gets <u>shorter</u>.
- During the downward movement the bicep muscle still <u>tenses</u> and <u>contracts</u> to control putting the dumbbell down. Instead of getting shorter, the muscle gets <u>stretched</u> and <u>lengthens</u> — this is an <u>eccentric</u> muscle contraction.

Bicep muscle

2) When a muscle gets stretched during an eccentric muscle contraction, extra <u>energy</u> is stored in the muscle (just like storing energy in an elastic band by stretching it).

3) This extra energy means the muscle can generate a <u>greater force</u> when it contracts normally.

4) The energy stored in an eccentric muscle contraction doesn't last forever — the <u>faster</u> the muscle can change between the two types of contractions, the more <u>powerful</u> the movement.

5) Plyometric training improves the <u>speed</u> you can change between the two types of contraction. It puts <u>a lot</u> of <u>stress</u> on the muscles and tendons though, so you need to do a really good <u>warm-up</u>.

6) Plyometrics is a type of <u>anaerobic training</u> and probably won't leave you out of breath. It <u>isn't</u> really needed for health-related fitness.

EXAMPLE: SQUAT JUMPS
Your quadriceps eccentrically contract when you bend your knees, and normally contract when you jump. Squat jumps improve the power of your quads and increase how high you can jump.

Running for a train — King's Cross training...

Plyometrics is complicated and it's going to take some time to get your head around. Just take it slowly and you'll get it. Oh, and in case you were still wondering, <u>fartlek</u> actually means '<u>speed play</u>' in Swedish.

Training Methods

You're on to the home straight now. Only this page left on training methods — you can do it...

7) Interval Training uses Fixed Patterns of Exercise

1) Fixed patterns of <u>high intensity</u> and <u>low intensity</u> exercise intervals are used in interval training.
2) For example, you might alternate <u>sprinting 200 m</u> with <u>jogging 100 m</u>, or in swimming, maybe alternate <u>sprinting</u> a set number of lengths with <u>resting</u> for a fixed length of time.
3) By doing <u>aerobic</u> exercise while recovering from <u>anaerobic</u> exercise, you push your heart and lungs more and improve your cardiovascular fitness loads — so it's good training for <u>team sports</u> like rugby.
4) But you need to <u>overload</u> to improve your fitness.
5) The downside is it's very <u>exhausting</u>.

OVERLOAD is achieved by increasing the proportion of time spent on the high intensity exercise, or by increasing the intensity (e.g. running faster).

8) Flexibility and Mobility Training Improves Suppleness

<u>Flexibility</u> and <u>mobility</u> training uses various <u>stretches</u> to improve your flexibility.
There are <u>three</u> different types of stretch you need to know about:

1) <u>STATIC</u> — A static stretch involves <u>gradually</u> stretching a muscle, and then <u>holding</u> the stretch position for a few seconds before relaxing it.

In an <u>ACTIVE</u> static stretch you use your <u>own muscles</u> to hold the stretch position. E.g. raising your leg in front of you to stretch your hamstring.

Stretched muscle

In a <u>PASSIVE</u> static stretch, you use <u>someone else</u> or a piece of <u>equipment</u> to help you hold the stretch position.

Stretched muscle

2) <u>DYNAMIC</u> — Dynamic stretching means slowly <u>increasing</u> the <u>range</u> of a movement that stretches the muscle.
E.g. swinging one leg forwards and backwards, making it swing higher each time.

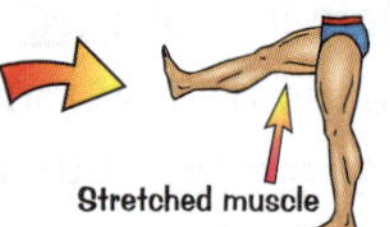
Stretched muscle

3) <u>PROPRIOCEPTIVE NEUROMUSCULAR FACILITATION (PNF)</u> —
For this kind of stretching you need to <u>contract</u> the muscle <u>before</u> you stretch it.
E.g. get a partner to raise one of your legs until you feel a <u>stretch</u> in your hamstring. Then <u>contract</u> your hamstring for a <u>few seconds</u> — your partner should hold your leg <u>firm</u> so it <u>doesn't move</u>. <u>Relax</u> your hamstring and get your partner to lift your leg slightly higher to <u>stretch</u> the muscle a <u>little bit more</u>.

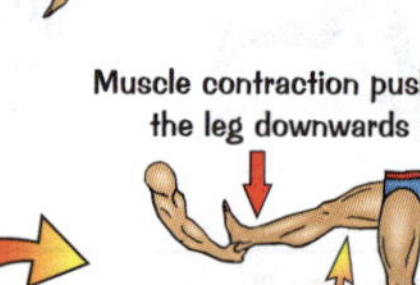
Muscle contraction pushes the leg downwards

Stretched muscle

9) Altitude Training Increases Cardiovascular Endurance

1) At <u>higher altitudes</u> the air pressure is lower — which means you take in <u>less oxygen</u> with each breath.
2) The body makes more <u>red blood cells</u> so enough oxygen can still be supplied to the body.
3) Athletes <u>train</u> at <u>high altitude</u> to increase their red blood cell count, then <u>compete</u> at <u>low altitude</u> while they still have some of these <u>extra</u> red blood cells. This means they have a much <u>better</u> oxygen supply to their muscles, which <u>increases</u> their ability to do <u>aerobic activity</u>.

Training Helps Improve your Mental Capacity

1) Training can not only help you to improve <u>physically</u>, but <u>mentally</u> too.
2) For a lot of sports and physical activities, there comes a point where you 'hit a wall'. You're <u>tired</u>, and <u>voices</u> inside your head start shouting at you to <u>stop</u> and <u>rest</u>.
3) By training, you can increase your ability to <u>keep going</u> even when you're tired.
4) You can also put <u>pressure</u> on yourself during training. This will help you be able to <u>cope with</u> competition pressure, which'll <u>improve</u> your <u>competence</u> and <u>performance</u>.

Altitude training takes you to the top...

Blimey, I thought training methods was never gonna end. There's a lot to learn, but stick with it and it'll soon sink in. Learn what each method does, and if it's good training for <u>aerobic</u> or <u>anaerobic</u> activities.

Training Plans

When I said p40 was the last page on training methods, what I meant was '...the last page — except p41'.

Training Should be Fun

As well as all those training methods there are loads of other fun activities and classes you can do to improve your fitness.

AEROBICS/AQUA AEROBICS — This involves doing aerobic exercises to music. It's good for improving strength, flexibility and cardiovascular endurance. Aqua aerobics is just aerobics in a swimming pool — it puts less strain on your joints so it's good for avoiding injuries.

DANCE EXERCISE — This is an aerobic workout that is based on dance moves. It's good for cardiovascular endurance.

BODY PUMP — This is a choreographed workout that combines weight training and aerobics. It's good for improving strength and cardiovascular endurance.

SPIN — This is a high intensity workout using exercise bikes which are set to different levels of resistance. It's good for improving both your cardiovascular and anaerobic fitness.

YOGA AND PILATES — Both yoga and pilates use a series of exercises and stretches that help increase strength and flexibility. Yoga exercises the whole body, while Pilates focuses more on the core torso muscles e.g. abdominals.

Training Plans Help Improve Specific Areas of Fitness

Now you've seen the different types of training, it's time to bring them together and create a PEP (see p36) Example: John is 15 and wants to improve at football. He wants a 12 week PEP and can train 3 times a week. He's tested his fitness by doing some 30 m sprints to test speed and Sargent jumps to test power. He's also done a Coopers 12 minute run test and has decided that he needs to improve his cardiovascular fitness. Here's a PEP John could use:

	Week One	Week Two	Week Three	Week Four
Session 1	Circuit training — focus on skills and sprinting	Circuit training — focus on skills and sprinting	Circuit training — focus on skills and sprinting	Rest
Session 2	Fartlek training	Fartlek training	Fartlek training	Rest
Session 3	Cross training — swimming	Spin class	Continuous training — running	Testing

When making a PEP try to remember:

Specificity — You need to match the plan to the person, the sport they want to play and what they want to improve.

Testing — so you can spot any areas you might want to work on, and monitor any improvement in your fitness.

Personal Eating Plan (PEP)
Mon: Cake
Tues: Cake
Wed: Cake
Thurs: Cake
Fri: Cake

Each training session will start with an appropriate warm-up and finish with a cool-down. The four week plan is repeated three times. Each week the intensity and difficulty is increased to cause overload and improve John's fitness. Every four weeks he rests and re-tests himself so he can monitor any improvements and adjust the difficulty and plan if it's needed.

There are Three Stages of Training for Competition

Most sports don't compete all year round, so athletes change their training plans depending on whether it's before, during or after the competition season — this is called periodisation.

1) Pre-season preparation — Anaerobic, aerobic and skills training — plus some extra strength training.
2) Competition/Peak Season — Compete regularly, while maintaining fitness and getting enough rest. Training can be planned so that you 'peak' at the right time (e.g. for key competitions).
3) Closed-season (out of season) — Recover from the strain of competition through rest and relaxation. Do some aerobic and strength training to maintain fitness and get ready for the next pre-season training.

I love it when a plan comes together...

Having a plan makes training a lot more effective. It means you can focus on the areas you want to improve, and check to see how you're doing. Get PEPed up and learn this lovely page before moving on.

Training Zones and Recovery

As you exercise, your muscles need <u>more oxygen</u> so your heart beats <u>faster</u> to get it to them. But, <u>only</u> if you're doing the AQA or Edexcel courses, do you have to draw <u>pretty graphs</u> like the ones on this page to show it.

Heart Rate — Heartbeats <u>per</u> Minute

1) Your <u>resting heart rate</u> is the <u>number of times your heart beats per minute</u> when at <u>rest</u> (i.e. when you're <u>not</u> doing any physical activity).

2) An adult's resting heart rate is normally between 60 and 80 beats per minute (bpm).

3) When you exercise, your <u>heart rate increases</u> to increase the <u>blood</u> and <u>oxygen supply</u> to your muscles.

4) The <u>more efficient</u> your cardiovascular system, the <u>slower</u> your pulse rate will be (either resting or exercising), and the <u>quicker</u> it will <u>return to normal</u> after you've been exercising.

5) You can find your theoretical <u>maximum heart rate</u> by subtracting your age from <u>220</u>.

6) The <u>difference</u> between your maximum heart rate and your resting heart rate is called your <u>working heart rate</u>.

> Working Heart Rate = Maximum − Resting

Training Zones — <u>get your</u> Pulse <u>in the</u> Target Zone

1) To <u>improve</u> your cardiovascular fitness and do <u>aerobic</u> training, you have to <u>work</u> your <u>heart and lungs</u> hard for <u>at least 15 minutes</u>.

2) To aerobically train, you need to make sure your heart rate is in the <u>target zone</u> (or the <u>aerobic training zone</u>).

> TARGET ZONE — between <u>60%</u> and <u>80%</u> of your <u>maximum heart rate</u>.

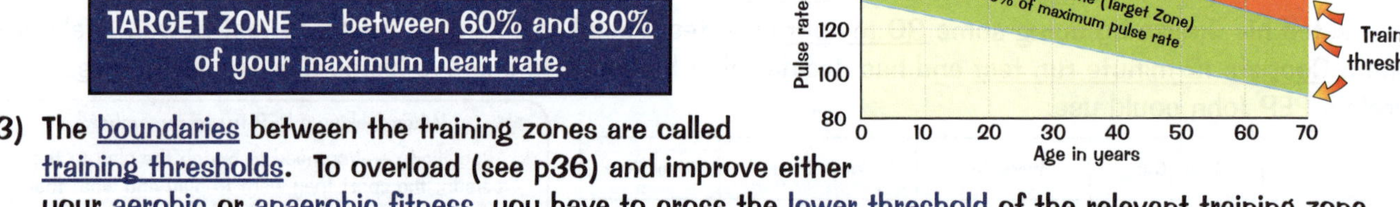

3) The <u>boundaries</u> between the training zones are called <u>training thresholds</u>. To overload (see p36) and improve either your <u>aerobic</u> or <u>anaerobic fitness</u>, you have to cross the <u>lower threshold</u> of the relevant training zone.

4) If you're just <u>starting</u> a training programme, you should be training with your heart rate near to the <u>60%</u> training threshold. <u>Professional athletes</u> will train <u>above</u> the <u>80%</u> threshold in the <u>anaerobic</u> training zone to improve their bodies' ability to <u>deal</u> with <u>lactic acid</u> (see p13).

Recovery Rate <u>Depends on</u> Fitness

1) It takes a while for your heart rate to return to <u>normal</u> when you stop exercising.

2) The length of <u>time</u> it takes for your heart rate to return to normal (your resting heart rate) is your <u>recovery rate</u>. The <u>fitter</u> you are, the <u>faster</u> your heart rate falls.

3) You can look at comparative fitness by using lovely <u>graphs</u> like these.

4) The fitter you are, the better your body will be at supplying your muscles with oxygen, so your body will take <u>longer</u> to reach its maximum heart rate.

5) Your recovery time not only depends on your fitness, but how <u>strenuous</u> the activity was too.

6) The more strenuous the activity, the more <u>anaerobic activity</u> your body will have been doing. You'll still need lots of oxygen when you <u>stop</u> exercising to get rid of the <u>lactic acid</u> build up.

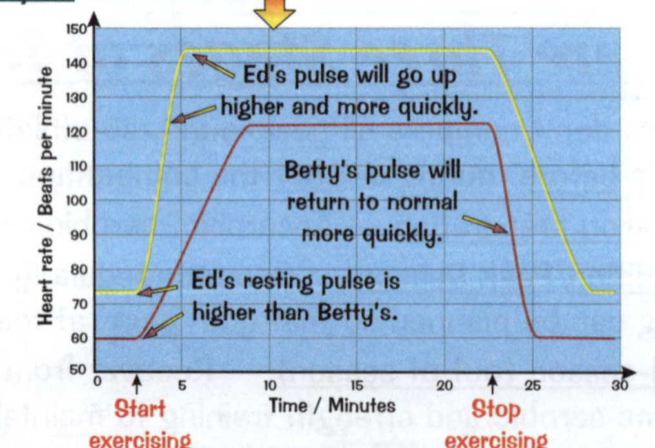

Ed's unfit.

Betty's fit.

Johnny Depp gets my heart in the target zone...

So the <u>fitter</u> you are, the <u>slower</u> your heart rate goes up, the <u>faster</u> it comes back down again. Got it? Good. Oh, make sure you know all the heart rate, training zone shenanigans too... it's all important stuff.

Types of Skill

<u>Skills</u> are all the things you use when you do an activity or play a sport — some are <u>simple</u>, like running, but others are more <u>complicated</u>, like serving in tennis, somersaults in gymnastics or singing the Welsh national anthem whilst on a unicycle. If you're doing the Edexcel or AQA courses you can miss this page out.

A *Skill* is Something You *Learn*

<u>Skill</u> is a word we use all the time. In PE, it's got a very fancy <u>definition</u>:

> A SKILL is a <u>learned</u> ability to bring about the <u>result</u> you want, with maximum <u>certainty</u> and <u>efficiency</u>.

So the main point is that a skill is something you've <u>got to learn</u>.
You can't be born with a skill, although you might learn it faster than other people.

There are <u>five</u> characteristics that make a movement skilful:

<u>PRE-DETERMINED</u> — With any skilled movement, you always have a <u>pre-determined result in mind</u> — you know what you want to do <u>before</u> you start. E.g. if you're passing the ball to someone in hockey you know what type of pass you're going to use and who you want to pass it to.

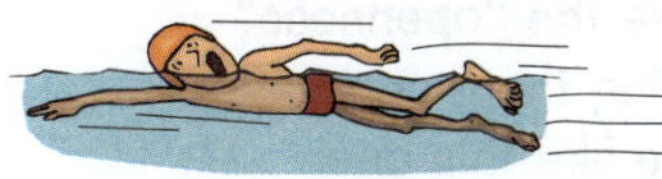

<u>EFFICIENT</u> — A skilled movement should be <u>efficient</u> and use the <u>minimum</u> amount of <u>energy</u>/<u>time</u>. E.g. a good swimming technique can help you swim faster and for longer.

<u>COORDINATED</u> — Skilled movements are <u>coordinated</u> — they use <u>two or more</u> parts of the body together to get the <u>maximum effect</u>. E.g. a vault in gymnastics requires good arm and leg coordination to produce the lift needed to get the technique right.

<u>FLUENT</u> — A skilled athlete is able to <u>flow</u> from one skilled movement to another, e.g. punch combinations in boxing.

<u>AESTHETIC</u> — On top of all this, skilled movements <u>look good</u>. In some sports, like gymnastics and figure skating, your skill is <u>judged</u> by the appearance of your movements. <u>Skilled</u> players make skilled movements and techniques <u>look easy</u>, while <u>less skilled</u> players and performers can look <u>awkward</u> and <u>uncomfortable</u>.

Fundamental Motor Skills — *Basic Skills like Running*

1) You tend to master a lot of <u>fundamental motor skills</u> at an <u>early age</u> when you learn to move about.

2) Fundamental motor skills tend to be <u>transferable</u> between many different activities.
    Just think of all the sports where you need basic skills like:

RUNNING	JUMPING	THROWING	CATCHING	KICKING	HITTING

3) You can <u>analyse</u> how good you are at some of these skills by doing simple tests. E.g. <u>timing how long</u> it takes you to run a set distance, or <u>measuring how far</u> you can <u>jump</u> or <u>throw a ball</u>.

4) When learning a <u>new sport</u> or <u>activity</u>, it's really <u>important</u> that you've mastered all the basic skills needed, <u>before</u> you attempt more complex ones.

I 'ave da skillz...

So any skilled movement should have a <u>pre-determined goal</u>, be <u>efficient</u>, <u>coordinated</u>, <u>fluent</u> and <u>look good</u>.
Make sure you can name the different <u>types</u> of <u>fundamental motor skill</u> and how to test them too.

Types of Skill

You can sort skills into different groups based on how much they are affected by other things. If you're doing the Edexcel courses you don't need to know about skills for the exam, so head straight to p47...

Skills are Open, Closed or Somewhere In Between

1) An open skill is one which is affected by many external factors. E.g. in golf, you can't just go up to the ball and take a swing, oblivious to what's going on around you. You need to consider things like the position of the hole, obstacles like trees, and the effect of the wind.

2) A closed skill is one hardly affected by the environment or external factors. E.g. in squash, you usually make the same movements — you don't need to change them for different conditions.

3) To confuse the issue, most skills actually fall somewhere in between. E.g. taking a football penalty — your environment doesn't change much, but you can alter your movement to change the speed and aim of the shot. So it's partly closed and partly open.

Most gymnastic events like the beam involve many different closed skills.

4) You can compare the "openness" of skills by putting them on a continuous scale like this one:

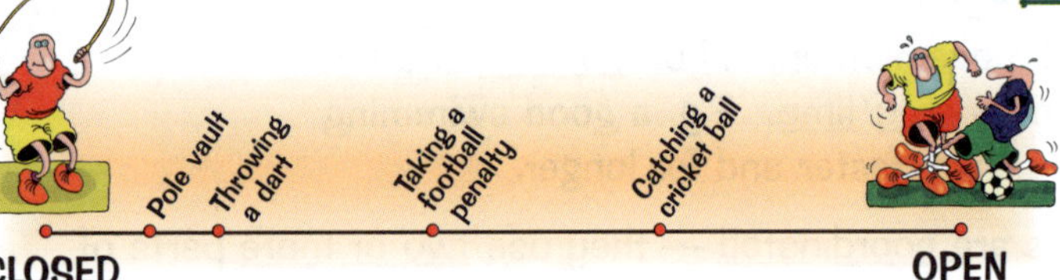

You Need to Decide What Skills to Use and When

In sports you have to make lots of decisions all the time. Whether you're a performer, leader/coach or an official — there's always something you have to make your mind up about.

PERFORMERS — make decisions about their individual performance.

1) You have to think about tactics and strategies 'on the go'. E.g. who to pass to next or when to 'close down' the opposition in invasion games — games where you enter your opponents half of the pitch like football or hockey. In target games (games where you aim to hit or throw something), e.g. golf, you decide what shot to play based the weather conditions and where the ball is. You also need to respond to what others are doing, e.g. reading a opponents tennis serve.

2) You also have to make decisions before you start, e.g. in activities like ice skating or gymnastics, you need to decide what to put in your routine when you're composing it. You also need to be creative when you're planning it so that it stands out from the other competitors.

COACH/LEADERS — make decisions that will affect the whole team.

1) You can plan different tactics and strategies to improve the performance of your team, e.g. choosing a formation, or making someone mark an important player on the opposing team so they can't have a big impact on the game.

2) You can also make decisions during the game, e.g. using a time-outs strategically in basketball to try and disrupt the flow of the game or choosing to substitute a player into a match.

OFFICIALS — have to make lots of decisions during a game.

They're responsible for making sure the rules are followed, and need to decide if they have been broken, e.g. deciding if a player is offside in football, or when there's a foul in netball.

Quick — get learning while there's skill time...

This whole open/closed lark is a bit weird. Basically — the more that doing a skill varies, and the more external factors matter, the more open a skill is. If you think pole vaulting is more open than throwing a basket ball — fine, as long as you can give reasons. In reality, it's pretty difficult to find any skills completely unaffected by any external factors — so most "closed" skills are actually a teeny bit open.

Learning and Developing Skills

Learning a new skill isn't easy. It takes <u>practice</u>, <u>practice</u>, <u>practice</u>... or <u>copying</u>... or <u>trial and error</u>...
If you're doing the Edexcel or WJEC courses, you don't need to know the stuff on this page.

There are Different Ways to Learn a Skill

1) <u>PRACTICE/REHEARSAL</u> — Practising means <u>repeating</u> a skill until you can do it. Try to make sure you've got a <u>trainer</u> or coach to help show you the correct technique to use. They'll also be able to make sure you're practising the <u>right skills</u> for your sport and sort out any problems in your technique.

There are <u>four</u> different types of practice you need to know about:

<u>WHOLE</u> — This means practising the whole technique in <u>one go</u>. It's good because you practice <u>all</u> the different parts of a skill at the <u>same time</u> — so you can get a <u>feel</u> for what the whole skill is like. Some skills are best learnt as a whole e.g. kicking a ball.

<u>PART</u> — If you're learning a <u>complex</u> skill it can help to <u>break</u> the whole skill down into <u>parts</u> and practice each bit <u>separately</u>, e.g. the ball toss and racket motion of a tennis serve. You can put all the individual bits together once you've got each one — so it's still important to know what the whole skill looks like.

<u>FIXED</u> — This means repeating the same technique in <u>one situation</u> over and over again — it's sometimes known as a <u>drill</u>.

<u>VARIABLE</u> — This involves repeating the technique in all of the <u>different situations</u> that you might need to use it in.

2) <u>COPYING OTHERS</u> — Another way to learn a new skill is to <u>watch others</u> doing it and then try to <u>repeat it</u>. It's a <u>good</u> way to learn a skill if you're <u>starting</u> a new sport because it shows you what the correct technique <u>looks like</u> and what to aim for. Even if you've got a grip of the basics, you can improve by watching <u>top athletes</u> or skilled <u>role models</u>, and trying to copy their techniques, e.g. copying different types of bowling action in cricket.

3) <u>TRIAL AND ERROR</u> — This is when you repeat a technique, but <u>change it slightly</u> each time to find out what works and what doesn't. It can be quite a <u>long process</u>, but it's a good way to improve and develop a skill, e.g. shooting an arrow or taking free kicks.

There are Different Ways to Develop a Skill

Once you've got the basics, you can <u>improve</u> and <u>develop</u> a skill or technique by increasing one or more of these things:

1) <u>RANGE</u> — e.g. once you know how to fire a bow in archery, you can try moving the target further away.

2) <u>DIFFICULTY</u> — e.g. adding a twist to a dive.

3) <u>CONSISTENCY</u> — this means being able to <u>reliably</u> do a technique, e.g. getting serves 'in' in badminton.

4) <u>PRECISION</u> — this means being more <u>accurate</u>, e.g. improving your aim in target games.

5) <u>CONTROL</u> — improving control will let you move on to more <u>advanced</u> versions of that skill e.g. going from controlling a football at jogging speed, to running speed.

6) <u>FLUENCY</u> — this means being able to perform a skill <u>smoothly</u> and <u>flow</u> from one technique to the next without having to stop and think in between, e.g. combinations in boxing.

<u>QUALITY</u> — By developing <u>all</u> the other aspects of a skill you will improve the <u>overall quality</u> of the skill too. Lovely.

Bobsleighers say 'packed ice' makes perfect...

There's quite a lot to remember on this page. Make sure you know how to <u>develop</u> a skill and the three types of learning — <u>practice</u>, <u>copying</u>, and ~~file and terror, pile and mirror, mile and error~~, <u>trial and error</u>.

Feedback and Guidance

To get better at a skill, you need to get feedback so you know what you're doing right and what you need to improve on. Remember, if you're doing an Edexcel course you can just jump ahead to the next page.

Feedback — Finding Out How You Did

Feedback can be either intrinsic or extrinsic:

> INTRINSIC — you know how well you did the technique because of what it 'felt' like.
>
> EXTRINSIC — someone else tells you or shows you what happened, and how to improve.

There are two parts of a skill or movement that feedback can focus on:

1) **KNOWLEDGE OF PERFORMANCE** — did you use the correct technique?

   Intrinsic feedback — e.g. you know you didn't kick the ball with the right part of your foot.

   Extrinsic feedback — e.g. a coach or trainer telling you which bits of the movement you did well, and which bits weren't so good.

2) **KNOWLEDGE OF RESULTS** — what was the outcome?

   This is usually extrinsic. It can come from coaches and trainers, e.g. a 400 m runner being told their time, or javelin thrower getting their distance.

   You can use all this feedback to work out your strengths and weaknesses and come up with an action plan to improve your performance.

Feedback can be Visual, Verbal or Manual

There are lots of different types of feedback and guidance a coach or trainer can give when you're learning or developing a skill.

1) **VERBAL** — This is the type of feedback you're most likely to get. Usually someone will watch you and then tell you what you did right and wrong and how to improve your performance.

   If you're giving feedback to someone, you need to think about what you're saying and how you're saying it.

   - Use a suitable volume — some people won't respond to being shouted at, especially if you're stood right next to them.
   - Make sure what you say is clear — use appropriate language and terminology for who you're talking to so they can understand what you're saying.
   - Project your voice if you're talking to a group of people, so they can all hear you.
   - Make sure your intonation (the tone of your voice) is right so you don't come across as rude or unhelpful.
   - Try to talk about some good things as well as the bad so the feedback is helpful and motivational.

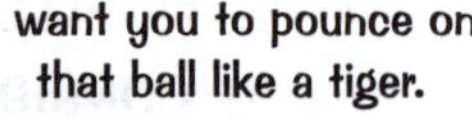

2) **VISUAL** — You can get lots of visual clues to help you perform a technique. E.g. a coach could use demonstrations or videos of your performance to show where you could improve your technique.

   You can also give and receive visual feedback during an activity, e.g. signalling where fielders should stand in cricket or making a gesture to encourage players to attack more in football.

3) **MANUAL** — This is when the trainer or coach physically moves your body through the technique, e.g. guiding your arms when you're practising a golf swing.

Verbal guidance is just what it sounds like...

There are quite a few terms on this page that you need to get you head around. Intrinsic means from you, extrinsic means from something external. Knowledge of performance is knowing how well you did something, knowledge of results is knowing what the outcome was. Feedback can be given visually, verbally or manually.

Motivation and Goal Setting

When the going gets tough — the tough get feedback and set SMART goals to help motivate them.
If you're doing an AQA course you don't need to worry about this page.

Feedback and Goal Setting can Help Motivate You

1) Motivation's about how keen you are to do something.
   It's what drives you on when things get difficult — your desire to succeed.

2) Just like feedback, motivation can be either intrinsic (from inside you) or extrinsic (from outside).

> INTRINSIC — You want to get involved as an official, player or leader because it's something
> you enjoy and you want to help — even if there are no prizes or rewards for taking part.

> EXTRINSIC — Maybe you want to do well as a player or leader because there's a big reward,
> e.g. prize money or publicity. Or maybe you're getting paid to referee a game so it can take place.

3) Good feedback can be a really good motivator — it can spur you on to work
   hard and really focus on the areas you want to improve.

Goal Setting is SMART

1) Goal setting means setting targets that you want to reach. They can be outcome goals,
   like winning the game, or performance goals like beating a personal best.

2) Goal setting can be a great motivator — it gives you something to aim for and helps ensure
   exercise adherence (a fancy way of saying it makes you stick to your training programme).

3) Short-term goals that you can reach quite quickly are steps on the way to a long-term one.
   It's important to have short-term goals so you don't get anxious
   or overwhelmed by a long-term goal, like trying to win an Olympic medal.

4) And if all that wasn't enough, reaching a goal can boost your confidence
   and can give you a sense of achievement.

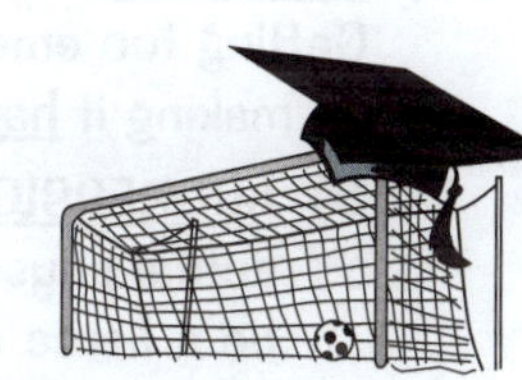

When you're setting targets — make sure they're SMART.

S → SPECIFIC: Say exactly what you want to achieve.
   1) Saying 'My goal is to be dead good at swimming' isn't very useful. It could
      mean anything — being able to swim very fast, for long distances, without your arm bands...
   2) You need to be specific and outline exactly what you need to do to reach your target.
      E.g. 'My goal is to swim 1000 m without stopping'.

M → MEASURABLE: Goals need to be measurable so you can know when you've achieved them.
      E.g. Good target — 'My goal is to run 100 m in under 12 seconds'.
      Bad target — 'My goal is to run the 100 m faster than I do now'.

A → ACHIEVABLE: You need to make sure your targets set at the right level of difficulty
      — too easy and it won't motivate you, too hard and you might give up.

'A' can also stand for 'agreed' — you should agree your goals with your coach.

R → REALISTIC: Set targets you can realistically reach.
   1) This means you have everything you need to fulfil your target.
   2) That could mean being physically able to so something.
   3) It could be that you have enough resources (time, money,
      facilities...) to be able to reach your target.

'R' can also stand for 'recorded' — you should keep track of your progress.

T → TIME-BOUND: Gives you a deadline for reaching your goal.
   1) You need a time limit to make sure your target is measurable.
   2) By meeting short-term target deadlines, you make sure you reach your long-term goals in time.

Goal setting — jumpers for goal posts...

This SMART rule to goal setting isn't just used in PE — it crops up everywhere, so it's worth while knowing
about. Make sure you know what SMART stands for, and that you can use it when you're setting targets.

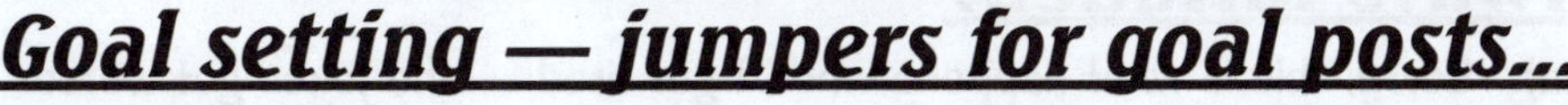

Fatigue and Stress

It's easy to get <u>stressed</u> doing a physical activity, which tends to have a <u>negative</u> effect on your performance. If you're doing the Edexcel or WJEC courses you don't have to know the stuff on this page for the exam.

Your Arousal Level shouldn't be Too High

To perform well you need to have the right arousal level. Arousal is about being <u>excited</u>, <u>keen</u> and <u>mentally ready</u> (or unready) to perform a difficult task.

1) If your arousal level is <u>low</u>, then you're not very excited and you're unlikely to perform well.

2) If you're <u>anxious</u> and <u>nervous</u> your arousal level is <u>too high</u>. You might become <u>tense</u> and 'stressed out' which can cause you to '<u>choke</u>' and be unable to perform skills you'd normally be able to, e.g. taking a penalty.

3) At the right arousal level you'll be <u>determined</u> and <u>ready</u> and should be able to perform your skills <u>well</u>.

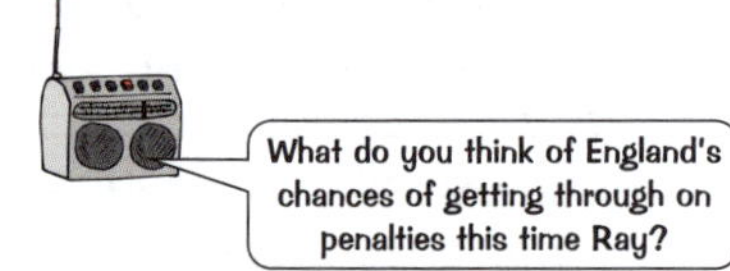

Stress and Fatigue Affect Your Skill Levels

Being <u>stressed</u> or <u>tired</u> means you're either over or under aroused, which can really <u>affect</u> your skill levels. There are lots of factors that affect your skill level, here are the ones you need to know about.

1) <u>PERSONALITY</u> — You can describe people's personalities by saying how <u>extroverted</u> (outgoing) or <u>introverted</u> (shy) they are — most people are somewhere in between.
   - Extroverts often choose <u>high excitement</u>, <u>fast</u> paced <u>team sports</u>, e.g. rugby.
   - Introverts tend to get <u>more nervous</u> and <u>stressed</u>. They usually choose <u>individual</u> <u>sports</u> that rely on <u>skill</u>, <u>precision</u> and <u>concentration</u>, e.g. a 5 km run.

2) <u>EMOTIONS</u> — When you get <u>stressed</u> and tired you get more <u>emotional</u>. Getting too emotional can make you <u>tense</u> and <u>anxious</u> or <u>aggressive</u> — making it <u>harder to concentrate</u> and perform the skills you need to use.

When Bruno got stressed you could see his nervous tick.

3) <u>AGGRESSION</u> — Aggression can either be indirect (e.g. hitting a tennis ball) or direct (where there's actual physical contact between two players). In some athletes, like swimmers, aggression can just be a fierce determination to win. Aggression can have <u>good</u> and <u>bad</u> effects. It's good if it's kept <u>under control</u> because it can help to <u>motivate you</u>. But as you get stressed or tired, it can become harder to control — which is bad if it means you <u>break</u> the rules or <u>injure</u> an opponent.

4) <u>BOREDOM</u> — You get bored when you're <u>mentally tired</u>. If you're doing a <u>repetitive</u> activity, e.g. practising a golf swing, it can quickly become <u>boring</u> and <u>tedious</u>. Your concentration level <u>drops</u> and you <u>stop performing</u> the skill well.

5) <u>FEEDBACK</u> — <u>Good feedback</u> can help <u>stop</u> you getting stressed give you tips on how to improve your performance and help <u>motivate</u> you. <u>Bad feedback</u> and <u>criticism</u> can get you <u>more</u> stressed, <u>harm</u> your confidence and make your <u>performance worse</u>.

Mental Preparation can Stop You Getting Stressed

<u>Mental preparation</u> is all about getting in the 'zone'. It can help you keep control of your emotions and <u>cope with stress</u> so you can perform at your best.

1) Many athletes follow <u>set routines</u> to <u>relax</u> them or get them '<u>pumped up</u>' for a performance.

2) <u>Focusing</u> on your <u>strengths</u> and imagining yourself performing well can help <u>focus</u> you on what you need to do and <u>raise your confidence</u>.

Why was the bike always fatigued?

...because it was two tyred (oh ha ha). Sorry, this is what happens when I get tired — the jokes get worse and I giggle like a baby monkey. Anyway, to help stop you worrying about 'fatigue and stress', <u>mentally prepare</u> by covering the page and then writing it all down. Keep trying until you can do it without peeking...

Preventing Injuries

There's a risk of injury whatever you're doing. You need to know how to make exercising as safe as possible.

Do a Risk Assessment Before You Start

1) Whenever you do an activity there's always a risk of getting injured — it could be from what you're doing, where you're doing it or who you're doing it with.

2) Normally the more challenging an activity is, the higher the risks involved in doing the activity.

3) You need to do a risk assessment, then do things to minimise the risks so the activity is as safe to do as possible for both yourself and others.

A Lot of Injuries can be Prevented

There are lots of things you can do before, during and after exercise to lessen your chances of getting hurt.

BEFORE THE ACTIVITY:

1) Before you do a new activity, you should assess your personal readiness by filling in a PAR-Q (see p33).

2) Warm-up before the activity, making sure you exercise the muscles you're going to use.

3) Use the right equipment — and check it's not damaged and in good condition.

4) Use the correct technique when lifting, carrying or placing equipment.
The techniques help stop you putting your back out or pulling a muscle.

5) Check for possible dangers in the area you're going to be exercising in.
- Officials should check competition areas and equipment.
- Leaders should check training and competition areas.
- Participants should check their own equipment.

E.g. you might need to check for dangers in:
Gymnasiums/sports halls/fitness centres
Playing fields
Artificial outdoor areas
Court areas
Outdoor adventurous areas e.g. mountain bike trails.

DURING THE ACTIVITY:

1) Play with people of the same:
- Size and strength — e.g. make sure you're in the right weight division, and not against someone who's twice your size.
- Skill level — don't try and play rugby against professionals on your first go.
- Gender — generally men are physically stronger and faster than women, so many sports often have separate women's and men's divisions.

2) Sports governing bodies usually set down rules and safety precautions to minimise risks to players of their sport. You should follow these rules, be sporting and try not to hurt an opponent.

3) Officials (e.g. referees) can ensure there's fair play and the rules and safety precautions are followed e.g. giving yellow or red cards for bad tackles in football.

4) Use the correct technique — e.g. safely tackling someone in rugby or hockey.

5) Make sure you're not wearing anything that could get caught (e.g. jewellery, watches).

6) Wear suitable footwear — e.g. wearing studded football boots or spiked running shoes makes you less likely to slip and injure yourself.

7) Use protective clothing/equipment where appropriate, e.g. mouth guards, cycling helmets.

AFTER THE ACTIVITY:

1) Cool-down properly.

2) Keep a good level of personal hygiene by washing afterwards to help stop minor infections.

3) Give yourself plenty of time to recover before playing again.

Sport — it's a risky business...

You'd think snooker was a fairly safe sport, but no. It can be a veritable blood bath — and I've seen it happen. The King's Head Snooker Tournament 2009 descended into chaos — 3 killed, 6 injured and 7 more still undergoing counselling. I've still got the scars from continuous prodding with a snooker cue.

Injuries — Types and Treatment

Now for the <u>gruesome</u> bit — injuries. You need know the different types of injury, and if it affects the hard tissues (bones) or the soft tissues (everything else). If you're doing the WJEC courses you can jump straight to the revision summary. For everyone else it's first aid, and then onto the squishy bits...

<u>Know</u> What to Do if Someone Gets <u>Injured</u>

Doing any kind of physical activity means you <u>might</u> get injured.
But there are some things you can do beforehand in case someone gets hurt:

1) Try and have a <u>first aider</u> present — sports competitions and events often hire members of the St John Ambulance in case of any injuries.

2) Make sure you have a well stocked <u>first aid kit</u> — and keep it near by you can get it quickly and easily.

3) Make sure you have access to a <u>phone</u> — if someone is seems seriously injured call **999** for an ambulance.

Most Sporting Injuries are to <u>Soft Tissue</u>

Your <u>soft tissues</u> are all the bits of you that <u>aren't bone</u> — muscles, skin, ligaments, tendons and stuff...
The most common injuries you can get are <u>cuts</u>, <u>bruises</u> and <u>swelling</u>.

1) <u>Cuts</u>, <u>grazes</u>, <u>blisters</u> and <u>chafing</u> can break the skin and cause bleeding.
Little ones will heal on their own but <u>large or deep cuts</u> will need <u>medical attention</u>.

2) <u>Bruising</u> is where your blood vessels get damaged — you bleed inside.

3) <u>Inflammation</u> is where the area around an injury <u>swells up</u> and is usually very sore.

<u>Inactivity</u> or <u>Overuse</u> can Injure Muscles and Tendons

1) If you never use your muscles, they'll eventually waste away, getting <u>smaller</u> and <u>weaker</u>. This is known as <u>muscle atrophy</u>.

2) And if you're not using your muscles, you won't be using your <u>tendons</u> either, so they'll get weaker too.

3) If your muscles and tendons are in this state, you're far more likely to <u>injure</u> or <u>strain</u> them, e.g. during strenuous activity, or by trying to lift heavy loads.

STRAIN

<u>Strained</u> (pulled) muscles and tendons are <u>tears</u> in the tissue — they're caused by sudden <u>overstretching</u>.

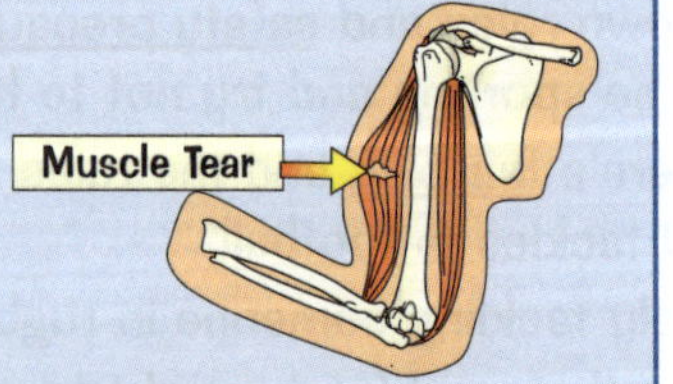

Pulled <u>hamstrings</u> and <u>calf muscles</u> are common injuries in loads of sports like football and cricket.

4) Whenever you <u>exercise</u>, you <u>damage</u> your muscles and tendons a little bit — it's what makes them <u>sore</u> the next day.

5) If you do <u>anaerobic exercise</u>, e.g. lifting weights, your muscles build up <u>lactic acid</u>.
This eventually causes them to become <u>tired</u> and <u>stop contracting properly</u>.
This is when you're most likely to <u>strain</u> and <u>injure</u> them.

6) Eventually this lactic acid build-up can cause your muscles to <u>stop working</u>, forcing you to stop exercising and <u>recover</u>. By regularly exercising anaerobically you can <u>increase</u> the amount of lactic acid your muscles can stand before this happens. Your body will also get better at <u>getting rid</u> of the lactic acid, which means you should be able to anaerobically exercise for <u>longer</u>.

Hard tissue! — Bless you — A soft tissue, please...

So the important things to remember from this page are the effects of <u>overuse</u> and <u>inactivity</u> on your muscles and tendons. Oh, and make sure you know the different types of soft tissue injury you might get, too.

Injuries — Types and Treatment

Here's some more stuff on <u>soft tissues</u> and how to <u>treat</u> them using RICE (no, not the food)... learn it well.
(Unless you're doing one of the WJEC courses of course... no tennis elbow fun for you I'm afraid.)

Joint Injuries can be Caused by Overuse...

<u>Continuous stress</u> on part of the body over a <u>long</u> period of time can cause all sorts of problems:

1) If you injure or overuse your tendons they can become <u>inflamed</u> and sore — this is called <u>tendonitis</u>. Tennis players can develop <u>tennis elbow</u> — a painful inflammation of tendons in the elbow. Golfers get a similar injury called, wait for it... <u>golfer's elbow</u>.

2) Long-distance runners can develop a nasty bone injury in the leg called <u>shin splints</u>.

3) You're more at risk of these types of injury if you <u>train too hard</u> or <u>don't rest</u> enough between training sessions.

... or Sudden Stress

1) <u>Sprains</u> are <u>joint</u> injuries where the <u>ligament</u> has been stretched or torn, usually because of violent twisting.

2) Joints can get <u>dislocated</u> as well. The bone is pulled out of its normal position — again, it's twisting that usually does it.

3) <u>Cartilage</u> can also be damaged. E.g. the cartilage of the <u>knee</u> can be <u>torn</u> by a violent <u>impact</u> or <u>twisting</u> motion.

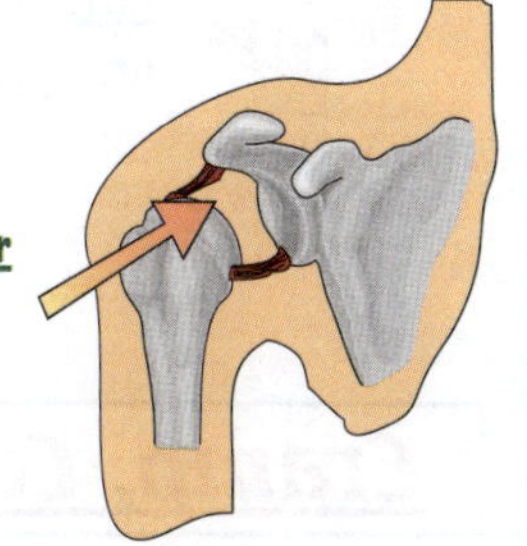

Dislocated shoulder
Humerus pulled out of joint.

Use the RICE Method to Treat Injuries

R   REST   ➡   Stop immediately and <u>rest</u> the injury — if you carry on, you'll make it <u>worse</u>.

I   ICE   ➡   Apply <u>ice</u> to the injury. This makes the blood vessels <u>contract</u> to reduce internal bleeding and swelling.

C   COMPRESSION   ➡   <u>Bandaging</u> the injury will also help reduce swelling. But <u>don't</u> make it so tight that you stop the blood circulating altogether.

E   ELEVATION   ➡   Support the limb at a <u>raised</u> level (i.e. above the heart). The flow of blood reduces because it has to work against gravity.

1) The <u>RICE method</u> is a good treatment for joint and muscle injuries like <u>sprains</u> or <u>strains</u>. It helps reduce pain, swelling and bruising.

2) As with everything, a little bit of <u>common sense</u> goes a long way. If the person has hurt their head, neck or spine — trying to elevate the injury is probably <u>not</u> a good idea.

If the RICE treatment doesn't work, try noodles...

You can gets lots of different types of rice — brown, white, long, short, sticky, egg fried, boiled, steamed, in a bag or as a pudding. But all of this is completely irrelevant, because what you need to know is that <u>RICE</u> stands for <u>rest</u>, <u>ice</u>, <u>compression</u> and <u>elevation</u>. And what the different <u>joint</u> injuries are too.

Injuries — Types and Treatment

You need to know four different types of <u>fracture</u> and how to treat some other common injuries that you might get when doing physical activity. Remember if you're doing a WJEC course you don't need to know this stuff.

Bones can Break in Different Ways

1) A <u>fracture</u> is a <u>break</u> in a bone. They're usually accompanied by <u>bruising</u> and <u>swelling</u>.
2) This is because a fracture also damages the <u>blood vessels</u> in or around the bone.
3) They'll also cause a lot of <u>pain</u> because of the damaged <u>nerves</u> inside the bone.
4) There are <u>four</u> types of fracture you need to know:

In a <u>simple</u> or <u>closed</u> fracture it all happens <u>under</u> the skin. The skin itself is alright.

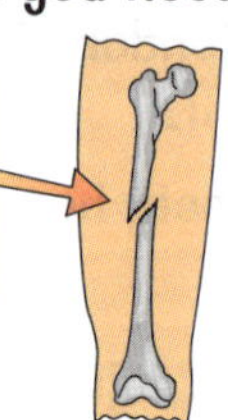

In a <u>compound</u> or <u>open</u> fracture the skin is torn and the bone pokes out. Urgghh.

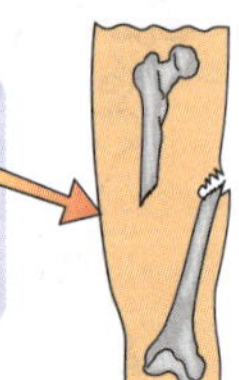

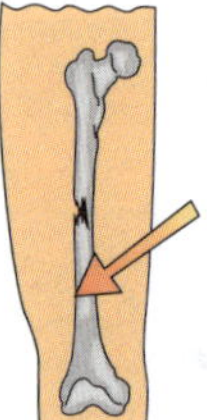

Greenstick fractures happen in young or <u>soft</u> bone that <u>bends</u> and <u>partly breaks</u>.

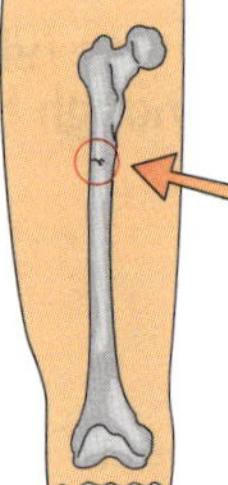

A '<u>stress fracture</u>' is a small <u>crack</u> in a bone. It's caused by <u>continuous</u> stress over a <u>long period</u> of time.

All other bone fractures are caused by a <u>sudden stress</u>.

Cramp, Concussion, Stitch — other Common Problems

CRAMP <u>SYMPTOMS</u>: <u>Involuntary</u> contraction of a muscle caused by a lack of <u>salt</u> minerals in the blood, or by a lack of blood flowing to a muscle. It's painful, but easy to treat.
<u>TREATMENT</u>: Just <u>stretch</u> the muscle and hold it like that, <u>massaging</u> it gently, until the muscle relaxes.

WINDING <u>SYMPTOMS</u>: Difficulty in <u>breathing</u>, pain in the abdomen, and you might feel sick. It's caused by a <u>blow</u> to the abdomen.
<u>TREATMENT</u>: Stop exercising, lean forward, and rub the affected area.

STITCH <u>SYMPTOMS</u>: A sharp pain in your side or abdomen. It's cause by the <u>diaphragm</u> cramping, so it can make breathing difficult.
<u>TREATMENT</u>: Stop exercising, take deep breaths, and breathe out slowly.

CONCUSSION <u>SYMPTOMS</u>: Unconsciousness, disorientation and memory loss. It's caused by a <u>blow</u> to the head.
<u>TREATMENT</u>: If unconscious, place the person in the <u>recovery position</u> (in this position, the head is tilted so that the airway won't be blocked by the <u>tongue</u> or by <u>vomit</u>) and get an ambulance. If they're conscious, keep the casualty under observation for 24 hours.

SHOCK <u>SYMPTOMS</u>: Pale, clammy skin. Rapid, weak pulse and breathing. The casualty may feel weak, faint, sick, dizzy or thirsty. It's caused by a drop in <u>blood pressure</u>.
<u>TREATMENT</u>: Call an ambulance, try to stop any external bleeding, reassure them and place them in the <u>recovery position</u>.

HYPOTHERMIA <u>SYMPTOMS</u>: Body temperature falls <u>below</u> 35 °C. Muscles go rigid, heart beats irregularly, casualty may fall unconscious.
<u>TREATMENT</u>: Steadily <u>raise</u> body temperature to 37 °C. Put them into <u>warm, dry clothing</u> or wrap them in a blanket. Give them <u>hot drinks</u>, and maybe a <u>warm bath</u>.

I don't ever remember having concussion before...

Well, it goes without saying that you need to learn everything on this page. Check you know the four types of fracture and for each condition or injury, practise scribbling down both the symptoms <u>and</u> the treatments.

Revision Summary — Section Four

Finally we made it. And I'm shattered. All this training malarkey seems like a lot of work. I don't know about you, but my little revision muscles are full of lactic acid and I need a rest to recover. But before that can happen there's just the small matter of these questions. So, take a breather, make a brew, and then have a go at answering them. As always, keep going 'til you can answer every one without cheating.

1) What does PAR-Q stand for?
2) Give two health checks you should do before exercise.
3) Write down three ways to test cardiovascular fitness.
4) Write down four tests for health-related fitness. Say what component of fitness each one tests.
5) How can you test a) agility, b) balance, c) coordination?
6) What does the Sargent jump test measure? How do you do it?
7) What are the five principles of training?
8) Explain why rest and recovery are important.
9) What does FITT stand for? Explain what each letter means.
10) Why is it important to warm up before and cool down after exercise?
11) What are the two things you need to consider when making a training plan?
12) Is weight training an aerobic or anaerobic activity?
13) What percentage of your maximum heart rate should you be at when doing continuous training?
14) Describe fartlek training.
15) Describe how circuit training works.
    Is it made up of aerobic activities, anaerobic activities or both types of activity?
16) Give one advantage of doing cross training.
17) What is plyometric training used to improve?
18) Describe interval training.
19) Describe three different types of flexibility training.
20) Explain how altitude training can improve an athlete's cardiovascular endurance.
21) What are the three stages of training for a competition?
22) What is the 'target zone' for doing aerobic training and what are 'training thresholds'?
23) Describe five different characteristics of a skilful movement.
24) List five different examples of fundamental motor skills.
25) What is the difference between an open and a closed skill?
26) Describe what's needed to be competent at something.
27) Give three different ways you can learn a new skill. Explain each one.
28) List six ways of developing a skill.
29) Explain the difference between intrinsic and extrinsic feedback.
30) Describe the difference between 'knowledge of performance' and 'knowledge of results'?
31) Name three different ways you can receive guidance and feedback.
32) What's the difference between an intrinsic and extrinsic motivation?
33) What do the letters in SMART stand for? Explain what each one means.
34) Give three ways fatigue and stress can affect your skill level.
35) Describe how can you prevent injuries a) before an activity, b) during an activity, c) after an activity.
36) What is muscle atrophy?
37) What's the RICE method?
38) What is a stress fracture? What causes it?
39) Describe the symptoms and treatment of a) cramp, b) concussion, c) shock.

Leisure Time and Access to Facilities

You get to do what _you_ want in leisure time, instead of doing your chores and stuff — it's _great_.
And people now have _way more leisure time_ than they used to — so it's even _more important_.

Leisure Time and Recreation are about Wants, not Needs

Most of our time is taken up by things that need to be done:

1) Social duties — going to school or work, and doing chores and things.
2) Bodily needs — mainly eating and sleeping.

In the time that's left, we can choose what we want to do. This is our leisure time.

> Leisure is free time, that you can use to do what you want. It might include a physical activity or sport.

Loads of people spend their leisure time doing some kind of recreation.

> Recreation is something you do in your leisure time to relax or be active.

DIFFERENCES BETWEEN SPORT AND PHYSICAL RECREATION:

1) Sports are more competitive — they have rules, and the aim is always to win. Sports have organised events and competitions.
2) Physical recreation and leisure activities are often non-competitive activities. You usually take part because of intrinsic rather than extrinsic motivations (see p47), e.g. you enjoy doing it. They're part of a healthy, active lifestyle, and are a way keeping up a sport or physical activity throughout your life.

People Have More and More Leisure Time

LEISURE TIME IS INCREASING — people have loads more than they did fifty years ago due to:

1) Less time working — the average working week is much shorter, and holidays are longer.
2) Technology helping with household chores — e.g. washing machines, vacuum cleaners, dishwashers. These machines have gradually become better, cheaper and more widely available.

This means people have more time to spend doing physical activity, and with the extra time to practise, their performance will generally be better too.

As people's leisure time increases, so does the demand for facilities and services to help fill that time. There's been huge growth in the 'leisure industry' in recent years — and it's likely to continue.

Both the Public and Private Sectors Provide Facilities

PUBLIC SECTOR FACILITIES:

1) Owned by local authorities and councils.
2) Usually run at a loss (funded by taxes).
3) Examples include: sports pitches, leisure centres, swimming pools and sports halls.

Sometimes local authorities will try and encourage certain groups to take part in physical activities — with things like special prices for OAPs, or mother-and-baby sessions.

These groups are called 'priority groups', 'user groups' or 'target groups'.

PRIVATE SECTOR FACILITIES:

1) Owned by companies or individuals.
2) Usually run to make money.
3) Examples include: sports stadiums (e.g. Wembley), tennis clubs, golf clubs, and health clubs.
4) They could also be voluntarily-run facilities, e.g. rugby clubs, or church halls.
5) National governing bodies for different sports will also fund facilities and training to try and find the next sports stars.

In my leisure time, I like to watch paint dry...

There are loads more leisure activities available today than there were 50 years ago — you've got loads to choose from. You can do almost any type of sport, from frisbee to canoeing to Tibetan yak riding, and most are dead easy to join in (except perhaps the last one — unless you live in Tibet and have a pet yak).

Leisure Time and Access to Facilities

The activities you choose to do are affected by lots of factors.

Where You Live Affects the Activities You Can Do

Your location will affect the physical activities you choose to do.

1) You might not need good facilities for many physical activities — but it definitely makes playing them easier. There are two sorts of facilities:

   - OUTDOOR FACILITIES — including pitches (e.g. for cricket), tracks (e.g. athletics) and facilities for water sports.
   - INDOOR FACILITIES — usually purpose-built buildings such as swimming pools and sports halls (used for loads of sports, like tennis, basketball, badminton and football).

2) It's no good having great exercise facilities if you can't get anywhere near them. Having easy access to sporting facilities means you're more likely to use them. If the facilities aren't near by, you'll need access to transport to get there — having a car, or good bus links to the facilities can really help.

3) The environment and terrain where you live will affect the activities you chose as well. If you live somewhere hilly like the Lake District, there's a huge amount of opportunity to do outdoor activities like hillwalking, mountain biking, rock-climbing or windsurfing. Because there's more opportunity, you're more likely to do these activities than someone who lives in the sprawling metropolis of Manchester.

4) The weather will affect your choices too. If it's cold and wet outside, you're more likely to choose an indoor activity like badminton than go and play volleyball on the beach. In hot, humid weather, you'll probably prefer a nice refreshing swim. Pollution in big cities might put you off doing outdoor activities too.

> The environment can also have a big effect on your performance too. If the weather's hot and humid you'll overheat faster and won't be able to perform as well. If you're exercising at high altitude, you breathe in less oxygen, so you'll get tired more quickly (see p40). The terrain can make a difference too — running 10 km will take you longer on a hilly route than a flat one.

Other Things Affect the Sports we Choose

There are lots of other factors that affect your participation in particular sports:

1) POLITICS — e.g. the Government might use a campaign to promote healthy, active lifestyles, or it might provide funding to build a new sports facility. It also decides which sports are taught in schools.

2) ACCEPTABILITY — Some sports are considered socially unacceptable by some people — e.g. they might object to off-road driving due to environmental concerns, or horse racing for animal welfare reasons.

3) CHALLENGE/DANGER — Many people are attracted to sports with an element of risk, like rock-climbing or motor racing. They wouldn't get the same stimulation and enjoyment from something like bowls.

4) MONEY — Learning an activity like skiing isn't easy for most people in this country. Sports like this are more popular with wealthy people who can afford to go abroad to ski. Similarly, some sports require expensive equipment which a lot of people can't afford.

5) LIFESTYLE — If you have a sedentary lifestyle (i.e. you don't do much physical exercise), you're more likely to choose a sport that isn't very strenuous. A sedentary lifestyle increases the risks of health problems such as heart disease or even obesity (see p27).

6) SKILL — You'll often enjoy a sport more if you're good at it, or if you want to improve.

7) STATUS — Some sports have a higher social status than others — e.g. polo is often associated with the wealthy and 'upper class', while a cheaper activity like football is considered more 'working class'.

Better make tracks — it's time to move on...

Make sure you know all the different factors that affect participation. You need to be able to understand why these things make a difference as well. Make a list of all the factors and learn them.

Influences on Participation

People can have an influence on the sports you take part in, whether it's your friends' opinions, your family's support or your own personal beliefs.

People Influence the Physical Activity You Do

Your family and friends can have a big influence on whether you do sport, and which sports you choose.

SUPPORT FROM YOUR FAMILY

1) Parents might encourage their children to take up sports.

2) Some sports need special clothing or equipment. It's usually parents who fork out the cash.

3) Many children can't easily get to and from sporting activities. They often rely on their parents to get them there.

PEER PRESSURE

1) Most people have a group of friends they spend most of their free time with. This group of friends is their peer group.

2) The attitudes of your friends will probably influence whether you like sport, and the sports you play. If all your mates play and like football, you'll probably play and like football. If your mates say that sport is rubbish and don't play it, you'll probably do less sport.

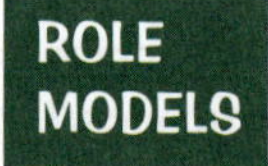

ROLE MODELS

People who excel in their sport can become role models for their sport and inspire people to be like them. This encourages more people to participate in their physical activity.

Race, Religion and Ethnicity can Affect Your Choices Too

1) Sometimes religious beliefs or cultural background can influence the physical activity you do.

> E.g. Many Muslim women keep their bodies covered up. This may mean they're less likely to participate in activities such as swimming because of the clothing that's expected to be worn.

2) Some religious groups organise their own sporting activities for members of their community or church — like football teams or cricket matches. This also makes their church more accessible to people in the local community, and might get them more involved with the church.

3) A lot of work has been done to try and make sure that people of all races have equal opportunities in sport and physical activity. However, some studies show that UK ethnic minorities are still less likely to participate in physical activity at all levels than white people.

4) Racism and racial abuse used to be a huge problem in sport. Campaigns against racism, such as the Show Racism the Red Card campaign, have helped to bring the problem of racism into the media. Unfortunately, incidents of racial abuse still go on, e.g. racist chanting at football matches.

Racial discrimination has affected sports all over the world — the apartheid system in South Africa banned black people from playing sport with white people. As a result of this, South Africa wasn't allowed to enter many international sporting events, including the Olympics — the 1992 Olympic Games in Barcelona were the first it was allowed to enter since 1960.

We're all under the influence...

I tried getting out of netball on religious grounds once. My teacher said if I was a actually a Jedi, I could use the force to throw the ball, but I was playing none the less. Anyway, lots of lovely influences to learn here — make sure you know them all before heading on over to the influences of gender.

Influences on Participation

There used to be a lot of <u>stupid</u> and <u>bigoted</u> views that stopped female participation in sport — held by both men <u>and</u> women. We've come on a long way, but things <u>still</u> aren't equal.

Women Used to be Discouraged From Doing Sport

Compared to nowadays, people used to think very <u>differently</u> about women in sport.

1) People thought physical activity was something to be done by <u>men only</u> and that it made women look very <u>unattractive</u>.

2) They believed that women could <u>harm themselves</u> by doing too much physical activity.

3) It was also thought women should wear 'respectable' clothing that covered their bodies up (e.g. long dresses). This meant that playing sport was very <u>uncomfortable</u>.

4) And to top it all off, people used to think women should look after the <u>home</u> and the <u>children</u> — this meant they didn't have the <u>time</u> or <u>energy</u> to play sport.

Greta felt awfully uncomfortable in goal.

Women's Sport Tends to Have a Lower Profile

Attitudes to women in sport are much better today. More and more women are playing sport because they aren't being held back. <u>Local authorities</u> often have <u>women-only</u> evenings at gyms and swimming pools as an incentive for women to join in. Despite all this progress, women's sport still faces problems.

<u>PROBLEMS FACING WOMEN'S SPORT</u>:

1) Many sports are still considered 'male only'.

2) Women are often <u>not allowed</u> to <u>compete</u> with men. This is even true in sports like <u>snooker</u> where factors like physical strength have no relevance. Showjumping is one of the few events where women <u>can compete</u> against men.

3) <u>Poor media coverage</u> — women's events usually have a <u>lower profile</u> than men's events.

4) <u>Less sponsorship</u> — companies want to sponsor the events with the most media attention, generally the men's events.

5) <u>Less prize money</u> — women's events usually have less prize money than men's events, even in sports where the women do get good media coverage.

6) <u>Fewer role models</u> for women — again, lack of media support is the main problem.

Women's Sport is Now Promoted

The UK <u>WOMEN'S SPORTS FOUNDATION</u> was set up in 1984. It aims to:

1) <u>Increase awareness</u> of the issues surrounding women in sport.

2) Help girls and women to get involved in sport at <u>all levels</u>.

3) Encourage <u>organisations</u> to improve sporting <u>opportunities</u> for women.

4) Challenge <u>inequality</u> in sport and seek to bring about <u>change</u>.

5) Raise the <u>profile</u> of British sportswomen.

Women Now Have More Opportunities in Sport

1) <u>Attitudes</u> to women in sport have changed in the last 25 years. Women now have more <u>equality</u>.

2) Women can now be <u>officials</u>, like <u>referees</u> and <u>umpires</u>.

3) Female <u>managers</u> and <u>directors</u> are more common — even in <u>male-dominated sports</u> like football.

4) <u>Sports teams</u> and <u>gyms</u> that are <u>only</u> for women are getting more girls <u>involved</u> in sport.

Only girls allowed...

So as you can see, women really do get a <u>rotten deal</u> when it comes to sport. Remember — the stuff at the top of the page about <u>attitudes</u> towards women is what many people <u>used to think</u>, it's <u>hopefully</u> not how many people think today. There's lots of juicy points here — learn 'em.

Influences on Participation

What your <u>body can do</u> can limit the physical activities you can do (that's not exactly the shock of the century). Whether it's your <u>age</u>, your <u>health</u> or a <u>disability</u>, it all has an affect...

Your Age can Limit the Activities You Can Do

1) Some sports are more <u>popular</u> than others with different age groups.

2) Most people aged 16-30 have <u>loads of choice</u> for physical activity, but more will choose to play tennis, say, rather than something like bowls.

3) People over 50 are more <u>physically limited</u> in the sports they can choose. They tend to do <u>less strenuous</u> activities like walking or swimming.

4) Some sports such as <u>weightlifting</u> and <u>long-distance running</u> can potentially <u>damage</u> a <u>young person's</u> body. Competitions in such activities often have a <u>minimum age restriction</u>.

Poor Health May Limit the Activities You Can Do

1) Becoming <u>temporarily</u> or <u>permanently ill</u> or <u>injured</u> can <u>stop</u> you from being able to do some physical activities.

2) However, some physical activities can actually <u>help</u> with particular medical conditions, e.g. <u>swimming</u>.

- Swimming is thought to be one of the best forms of exercise for <u>asthma suffers</u>.

  Some <u>asthma attacks</u> are brought on by breathing in <u>cold</u>, <u>dry air</u> during physical activity. The atmosphere at a swimming pool is usually <u>warm and damp</u>, so they're less likely to have an attack while exercising.

- Swimming's also a great way of exercising for people who have <u>joint problems</u> — the water helps <u>support</u> the body, which puts <u>less pressure</u> on the joints.

Disability will Influence You Too

1) Having a <u>disability</u> can limit the physical activities you can do.

2) The <u>opportunities</u> in sport and <u>access to sporting facilities</u> for disabled people used to be few and far between.

3) Nowadays, there are many schemes set up to give disabled people more opportunity to exercise and take part in activities within their physical limits.

4) Disabled sporting events are now given a lot more <u>media coverage</u> than they once were. The Paralympics are now given extensive <u>media coverage</u>, like the Olympics.

5) This media coverage is helping to <u>change people's attitudes</u> towards disability and sport.

6) It's also helping create many more <u>disabled role models</u> (like <u>Dame Tanni Grey-Thompson</u> and <u>Ellie Simmonds</u>), which encourages more disabled people to get active.

I hope I'm still break dancing at 60...

Age-wise it's not like you get to 50 and that's the end of the road. The oldest Olympic medallist was a Swedish chap, who won a silver for shooting at the age of 72. OK, so shooting isn't the most physical of activities... but still pretty darn impressive. Almost as impressive as the number of influences here...

Influences on Participation

School, school, school... the best days of your life, so they say.

PE Teachers Can Affect Your Attitude Towards Exercise

1) A good teacher can build up your confidence, identify your strengths and potential, make activities enjoyable and provide quality coaching — whereas a bad teacher can put you off PE for life.

2) PE teachers who run after-school or lunchtime clubs are trying to encourage you to get more involved in sports — and they're making an effort too.

3) Your school should promote and give you the chance to get involved in health awareness programmes.

And Your School Facilities Have an Influence Too

1) It's not just PE teachers that affect your enthusiasm — your school's facilities make a big difference too.

2) If your school has a wide range of good quality facilities (like a gym, swimming pool, all-weather pitches and playing fields), then you'll have lots of opportunities to try different activities. The more activities you try, the more likely you are to find ones you like, or are really good at.

3) Unfortunately, not all schools have these lovely facilities. A lack of space or money could mean you're restricted to one measly, molehill-ridden field, with everyone in school wanting to use it at once.

4) But even if your school doesn't have many facilities itself, it can still give you opportunities to try new sports by organising trips to places such as dry ski slopes, ice rinks or outdoor activity centres.

Links with Clubs can give more Opportunities

1) If your school has a link with a club (e.g. a football club), it can give you access to professional coaching and the chance to get even more involved with the sport.

2) Getting involved with a local club can give you the chance to try out new things — you might be able to coach a junior team, or help organise club events. This sort of thing might also help you to have a career in sport.

3) Links with a club might also mean you're able to train for qualifications that you wouldn't be able to through your school.

There are Loads of Different Pathways to Follow

1) Performing isn't the only way to take part in sporting activities — you can be a leader, a coach, an organiser, a choreographer or an official. You can also get involved by volunteering. (See p4-5)

2) You can't just turn up one day and expect to be made the referee — you have to work towards it. But you can start doing this through your school or a club.

3) There are lots of different pathways you can take. A pathway is a set of steps showing how you can progress through a sport, from a beginner to competition level (or official etc.). At each step, there are more complex and challenging tasks you have to complete.

4) In some activities, these pathways can lead to official qualifications, accreditations or awards.

5) A typical pathway might look something like this:

1) Doing an activity or sport regularly. → 2) Taking part in school or community sporting events. → 3) Reaching a really high standard of performance, and entering national competitions.

OR

3) Deciding to become a coach or official and working towards accreditation.

Make use of your school's facilities...

You spend about 15,000 hours of your life in school — so it stands to reason that it has a big influence on whether you like something. There are all sorts of factors though — teachers, facilities and activities.

Government Schemes

The <u>Government</u> doesn't want a country filled with obese heart disease victims.
That's why it sets up <u>schemes</u> and <u>initiatives</u> to get young people more active.

Government Schemes Encourage Physical Activity

1) The Government believes that schools have an important role to play in generating <u>interest in sport</u> —
if you <u>enjoy</u> sports at school you're more likely to take them up when you leave.

2) The <u>National Curriculum</u> for PE sets out what teachers must teach. It's designed to <u>encourage</u> young
people to enjoy sports, both <u>in</u> and <u>out</u> of school, and to understand that physical activity is a vital part
of a <u>healthy, active lifestyle</u>.

3) PE lessons are supposed to help you develop a wide <u>range of skills</u> like <u>tactics</u>, <u>planning</u>, <u>goal setting</u> and
<u>decision-making</u>, as well as improving your <u>physical skills</u>.

4) You should also have the chance to try out roles other than performing, such as <u>leading</u> or <u>officiating</u>.

5) By developing the <u>skills</u> and learning about the <u>processes</u> and <u>decisions</u> made by people in different roles
(see p4-5) you're more likely to stay <u>interested</u> and <u>keep doing</u> an activity.

6) In addition to the National Curriculum, the Government has also produced schemes like <u>PESSCL</u>, <u>PESSYP</u>
(see next page) and the <u>Healthy Schools Policy</u> (see below). These <u>set out in detail</u> the Government's
plans for getting young people healthy and active.

The Healthy Schools Policy and PSHE Teach about Health

The <u>Healthy Schools Policy</u> is a scheme set up by the <u>Government</u> as part of the national health agenda.
It tries to encourage pupils to have a <u>healthy, active lifestyle</u>. It teaches you about <u>eating healthily</u>,
<u>exercise</u> and your <u>emotional needs</u>, so you can make informed decisions about your lifestyle.
Different bits of the policy are taught in lessons like <u>PE</u>, <u>Food Technology</u> and <u>PSHE</u>.

Healthy Eating

1) Schools should encourage you to <u>eat healthily</u>. As well as providing <u>healthy food</u>
at lunch and breaktime, they should also <u>teach</u> you about <u>balanced diets</u>.

2) The <u>Whole School Food Policy</u> means that <u>everyone</u> (parents, staff and students)
is involved in planning <u>healthy meals</u>.

3) You also need to know about <u>health initiatives</u> — like eating <u>five</u>
portions of <u>fruit</u> and <u>veg</u> every day.

An apple a day...
...still means you need to eat four
other portions of fruit or veg.

Physical Activity

1) Schools are supposed to <u>promote physical activity</u>.

2) You must have <u>two hours</u> of <u>structured physical activity</u> a week (i.e. your PE lessons) but you should
really aim to do <u>one hour</u> of <u>physical activity</u> or <u>sport</u> a day.

3) Your school should encourage you to take part in <u>extracurricular sports</u>.

Emotional Health and Wellbeing

1) Schools have to consider <u>vulnerable students</u> (ones who might need more <u>support</u> because of their
<u>gender</u>, <u>race</u>, <u>religion</u>, <u>disability</u>, <u>sexuality</u> or <u>class</u>) and make sure they can have a <u>healthy, active lifestyle</u>.

2) This means schools have to make sure that <u>everyone</u> can take part in <u>PE lessons</u>, and that nobody is
<u>discriminated</u> against for any reason.

3) All schools should have an <u>Anti-Bullying Policy</u> and <u>reward schemes</u> for good behaviour. A school's
<u>pastoral system</u> (i.e. looking after your <u>personal</u> and <u>social well-being</u>) should be <u>confidential</u>.

Does a chocolate orange count as one of my five-a-day?

A lot of this page is just <u>common sense</u> really — I expect you know that you need to <u>eat healthily</u> and
<u>exercise</u> to have a <u>healthy, active lifestyle</u> (the name says it all really). It's not the most exciting page,
but you need to make sure you know about all the different bits of the <u>Healthy Schools Policy</u>.

Government Schemes

And there's more... PESSYP and PESSCL are the main Government strategies.
But there are lots of other initiatives that have branched off from these.

PESSCL — PE, School Sport and Club Links Strategy

1) The PESSCL strategy was set up by the Government in 2003 to get young people doing more sport —
a key target was to give at least 85% of school children access to two hours per week of quality physical
activity in school by 2008, which was actually achieved a year early, in 2007.

2) It encouraged links between schools and sports colleges — and funding was provided for this.

3) The PESSCL strategy also supported other schemes like Specialist Sports Colleges (SSC),
the gifted and talented programme, Step into Sport, the TOP LINK programme,
School Sport Partnerships (SSP) and other school, club and community links.

SPECIALIST SPORTS COLLEGES (SSC) — schools that really focus on
PE and sport. They're given funding from the Government for equipment
and facilities, and are expected to work with local primary schools and
their local community to help them develop sports too.

GIFTED AND TALENTED PROGRAMME — a programme designed to help elite
young athletes achieve their full potential. It aims to identify high flyers in PE
and give them the support and funding they need to make it to the top.

STEP INTO SPORT — aimed at 14-19 year olds. It encourages them
to be sports leaders and volunteers, both now and in the future.

TOP LINK PROGRAMME — a programme set up to develop links between schools.
It helps 14-16 year olds set up sport or dance festivals for their local primary schools
or special schools. It's supposed to develop leadership and organisational skills.

SCHOOL SPORT PARTNERSHIPS (SSP) — groups of schools that work together to improve PE skills.
Specialist Sports Colleges, other secondary schools, primary schools and special schools all share
resources and knowledge — it gives children in these schools more opportunities.

PESSYP — PE and Sport Strategy for Young People

1) The PE and Sport Strategy for Young People (PESSYP) was set up in 2008 to replace PESSCL.
It builds on the PESSCL strategy, with the same overall aims of increasing the amount and quality of
sport schoolchildren do.

2) Like PESSCL, the first aim is for everyone aged 5-16 to have two hours of quality physical activity a
week in school time. But in this new strategy, all 5-19 year olds should also be given the opportunity
to do at least three hours of extracurricular sport every week — this is known as the 'Five Hour Offer'.
PESSYP also aims to increase coaching opportunities for older students.

3) New schemes set up as part of the PESSYP strategy include a National School Sport Week,
a Young Ambassadors programme and a National Talent Orientation Camp — more of these
last two on the next page...

So many acronyms — PESSCL, SSC, SSP, TARDIS...

There are lots of different schemes on this page — make sure you know all the names and what they do.
Remember, PESSYP was set up to replace PESSCL, and build on what it had started. But they all have a
similar purpose — to get young people more involved with sport. That's the aim of the game.

Sport Organisations

One more desperately exciting page to do with getting young 'uns off the sofa and doing exercise.
Two organisations that do lots of stuff towards this are Sport England and the Youth Sport Trust.

Sport England Want Everyone to get Into Sport

1) Sport England is a Government organisation that provides funding for various sports schemes and programmes. Some of the money comes direct from the Government, some is from the National Lottery.

2) It provides funding to organisations such as UK Sport to develop promising UK sporting talent.

3) It also works closely with the Youth Sport Trust on providing sporting opportunities for young people.

4) The key aims are summarised in its motto 'Start, Stay and Succeed' (also called 'Grow, Sustain, Excel').

START Increase participation in sport in order to improve the health of the nation, with a focus on priority groups.

Priority groups are groups of people that are known to take part in less physical activity than others e.g. women.

STAY Keep people in sport through an effective network of clubs, sports facilities, coaches, volunteers and competitive opportunities.

SUCCEED Create opportunities for talented performers to achieve success.

5) The Sports Council for Wales (SCW) is an organisation that supports and funds sport in Wales. Its aims include getting 90% of Welsh secondary school children to do 60 minutes of activity five times a week (the 5×60 initative).

The Youth Sport Trust Works to get Children Active

1) The Youth Sport Trust (YST) is a charity that does loads of work aimed at getting children involved in sport. It is heavily involved in delivering the Government's PESSYP strategy. It runs a range of programmes to get different people involved in physical activities in different ways.

2) As well as the Top Link Programme (see prev. page), it runs a Top Sportsability programme to provide opportunities for disabled children to join in sporting activities with non-disabled children.

3) There's also the Top Activity Programme (also called Active Kids). This uses less common sports to encourage children to take part in physical activity — things like cheerleading and martial arts. This programme takes place out of school hours.

4) As part of PESSYP, it started the Young Ambassadors programme — a scheme to allow 16 and 17 year olds who are either really good at sport or have good leadership skills to act as role models for younger athletes.

5) Also as part of the new PESSYP, it runs an annual National Talent Orientation Camp (NTOC) for gifted and talented athletes. It's a camp where young athletes get to train and meet successful sporting role models, like Olympic medallists.

My PE teacher was such a schemer...

Phew! You'll be deeeelighted to know that there's no more stuff on sports schemes and initiatives after this page. So just make sure you know how the ins and outs of the various Government schemes, what organisations are involved in delivering them and where all the money comes from.

Levels of Participation in Sport

You can <u>take part</u> in a sport at <u>different levels</u> — from being forced, kicking and screaming, to do it in PE at school to <u>dedicating your life</u> to it and winning an Olympic gold medal.

The Sports Participation Pyramid (of joy)...

Not every footballer in the world is making millions playing in the Premier League (I wish...).

There are <u>four different levels</u> of participation within a sport, and the <u>number</u> of people participating gets <u>smaller</u> at each increasing level. You can show this using a <u>pyramid</u>:

STAGE 1 — FOUNDATION

1) You may not <u>understand</u> all the <u>rules</u> at this stage. You'll be developing <u>basic skills</u> needed for the sport.
2) Most people are normally at this level while at <u>school</u>.

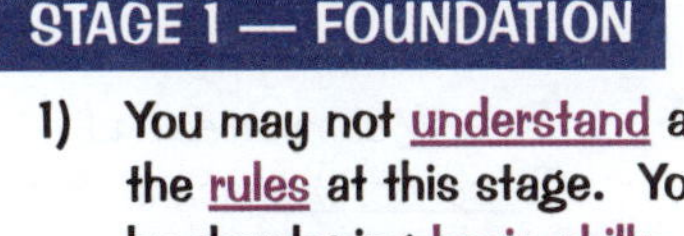

STAGE 2 — PARTICIPATION

1) You <u>choose</u> to do a sport <u>regularly</u>.
2) You're <u>competent</u> at your chosen activity.
3) Your reasons could be anything from <u>socialising</u>, <u>health</u>, <u>fitness</u> or <u>fun</u>.
4) You could join a <u>sports club</u> or just play in your <u>own leisure time</u>.

STAGE 3 — PERFORMANCE

1) This is when you're <u>training seriously</u> and are <u>committed to improving</u> your <u>sport-related skills</u>.
2) This might mean playing for a team or club where you receive some <u>coaching</u>.
3) You're able to <u>perform</u> and <u>compete</u> at a club or <u>regional level</u>.

STAGE 4 — ELITE

1) Right at the top of the pyramid are the <u>highly-skilled</u> elites who have reached a level of <u>excellence</u>.
2) At this level you're competing in <u>national</u> and <u>international</u> competitions, and can be an <u>amateur</u> or <u>professional</u> athlete.

There are Three Main Types of Competition

A lot of sport's about competition, let's face it. These are the main ways competitions are organised:

1) **LEAGUE** — E.g. football divisions. Each team or player plays against <u>all</u> the others at least once (often twice — home and away). They get <u>points</u> for winning or drawing a game. The winner is the player or team with the most points at the end of the season. Leagues are a very <u>fair</u> way to run a competition, because they reward <u>consistency</u> over a long time. The trouble is they may take <u>too long</u>, and if there are too many people or teams they may have to be divided up into smaller leagues.

2) **KNOCK-OUT** — E.g. tennis tournaments. Knock-out competitions are played in <u>rounds</u>, with each player or team playing one game per round. They go through to the next round if they win, otherwise they're out of the competition. Knock-outs are <u>easy to organise</u> and <u>quick</u> to run, but they're not as fair as you <u>only get one chance</u>. On the other hand, they're more <u>exciting</u> to watch and take part in.

3) **LADDER** — E.g. squash competition ladders. The players are listed on a ladder. Each can <u>challenge</u> a player higher on the ladder, but only up to a certain number of rungs higher. If they beat them, they <u>take their place</u> on the ladder. This is no good for team sports, and can be demoralising for <u>new players</u> who must start at the <u>bottom</u>.

Some competitions are made up of a <u>mixture</u> of these — and some even have <u>qualifying stages</u> (where you have to reach a <u>certain level</u> before you even get to the <u>main competition</u>).

I'm a foundation-level sumo wrestler...

Just remember that the <u>higher</u> up the pyramid you go, the <u>fewer</u> athletes there are at that stage.
Think about it — lots of people can <u>run</u> or <u>swim</u>, but very few of them compete in the <u>Olympics</u>.

Sports Careers

It's dead important to know the difference between an <u>amateur</u> and a <u>professional</u>. It's all about <u>money</u> — professionals get paid but amateurs don't. You only need this page if you're doing an AQA course.

Pros do it for Money — Amateurs for Love

<u>AMATEURS</u> — <u>don't get paid</u> for playing sport — they do it as a <u>hobby</u> because they like it.

<u>PROFESSIONALS</u> — <u>get paid</u> for playing their sport — it's their <u>full-time job</u>.

1) Some sports are <u>totally amateur</u>, e.g. rowing.

2) Others have professionals and amateurs who compete <u>separately</u>, e.g. boxing.

3) Others are <u>open</u> — everyone competes against everyone else, e.g. golf.

The <u>Olympics</u> were originally only supposed to be for <u>amateurs</u>. But people started to <u>bend</u> the rules — getting paid for playing their sport, but still competing as <u>amateurs</u> so they could take part in the Olympics.

It became <u>impossible</u> to decide who was a true amateur, so the word 'amateur' was dropped from the Olympic rule book. <u>Governing bodies</u> and the <u>IOC</u> (International Olympic Committee) now decide who can compete in the Olympics (see p68).

Money from <u>TV</u> companies and <u>sponsorship</u> means that professional athletes can now earn millions of pounds a year.

'Mole-in-pic'

Some Amateurs Find Ways of Getting Paid

Amateur athletes often want to find ways to train full-time, <u>without</u> being classed as professionals.

1) <u>SCHOLARSHIPS</u> — Colleges let athletes train <u>full-time</u> for free, without doing much actual studying.

2) <u>TRUST FUNDS</u> — Prize money is paid into a <u>trust fund</u>. Athletes can take <u>living expenses</u> from the fund during their career — and get the rest when they retire.

3) <u>SPONSORSHIP</u> — E.g. athletes get paid for wearing a company's <u>logo</u> on their clothing (see p65).

4) <u>'EXPENSES' PAYMENTS</u> — These are often much <u>more</u> than what the athletes actually spend.

5) <u>TOKEN 'JOBS'</u> — Athletes can be given '<u>jobs</u>' where they don't have to do anything, so can train full-time.

6) <u>GIFTS</u> — Things like cars could be given as <u>presents</u>, and then sold.

7) <u>ILLEGAL PAYMENTS</u> — Nothing fancy here. Just take the cash and keep <u>quiet</u>.

You Don't Have to be an Athlete to Have a Career in PE

If you're <u>interested</u> in PE but don't fancy being a <u>professional sportsperson</u>, there are other <u>careers</u> you could go for.

1) <u>PE teacher</u> (see p59)

2) <u>Coach</u> or <u>trainer</u> (see p5 and p46)

3) <u>Sports physiotherapist</u> — diagnosing sports injuries and treating them through manual therapy and exercises. Sports physiotherapists also advise people about how to avoid such injuries in the future.

4) A job in <u>sports management</u> — perhaps being involved in running schemes like the ones on pages 61-62.

Would anyone like to sponsor me?

In the olden days, most sports didn't let amateurs and professionals compete together — but <u>cricket</u> did. Amateurs were '<u>gentlemen</u>', and professionals '<u>players</u>'. The teams were usually a mix of both — but once a year they played against each other in the '<u>Gentlemen and Players</u>' match.

Sponsorship

Sponsorship exists to give good <u>publicity</u> to the sponsors. Sponsorship funds sports, teams or individuals in part or in full. The more <u>famous</u> the sport, team or individual, the higher the payout. If you're doing the Edexcel or WJEC courses you can skip this page.

Everything is Sponsored, from the Team to the Ball

If people are going to <u>see</u> it, companies will slap their <u>name</u> on it, whether it's a person, team, league, stand, trophy, mascot, badge, or ball. This means big bucks for the <u>famous few</u>.

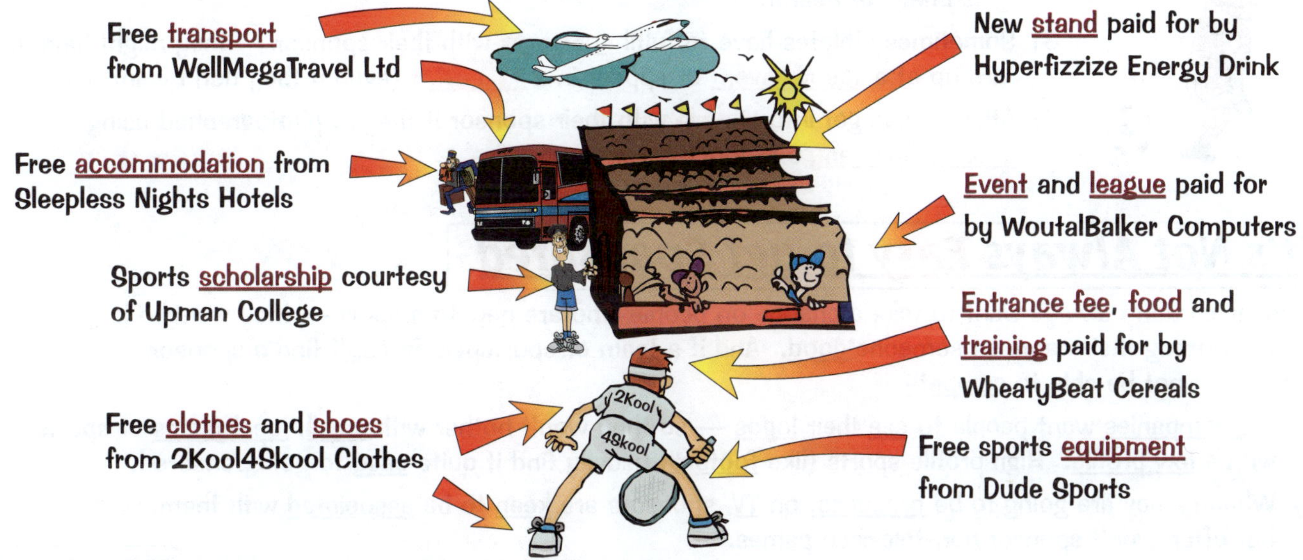

Sponsorship can be Good for Sport

1) Sponsorship pays for full-time sportspeople to <u>train</u> and <u>compete</u> — they can focus all their time on training, and not have to worry about money or another job.

2) It also pays for <u>events</u>, <u>leagues</u> and things like <u>stadiums</u>.

3) It <u>promotes</u> development of up-and-coming sports stars — people who might have struggled to get noticed or accepted into the big leagues without a sponsor.

Sponsors get a lot out of Sponsorship Too

Why do sponsors give away all that dosh? Read on and learn their devious ways...

1) <u>FREE ADVERTISING</u> — See a good player using it and <u>you'll want to</u> use it.

2) <u>IMAGE</u> — The company becomes associated with <u>winners</u>.

3) <u>SCHOLARSHIPS</u> — Some <u>universities</u> and <u>colleges</u> offer places (at discounted grades) to students who excel at particular sports. In return universities gain <u>prestige</u> for sporting excellence.

4) <u>TAX AND HOSPITALITY</u> — Sponsors <u>don't</u> usually have to <u>pay tax</u> on the money they spend on sponsorship. They also get <u>free tickets</u> to the events they sponsor, which they can use to impress clients and employees.

5) <u>AREN'T THEY NICE</u> — Companies often sponsor <u>charity</u> and <u>local events</u>. Whether this is out of the kindness of their hearts or to <u>improve</u> their <u>corporate image</u> is by the by.

CGP CGP CGP CGP (CGP — Official Sponsors of page 65)...

Sponsorship is a good way of getting money into sport. On the surface, it looks like a win-win situation for everyone, but it does have downsides (see p66 for the dark side of sponsorship). Make sure you know <u>who</u> gets <u>what</u> out of it. And <u>memorise</u> all the ways that companies get their names into sport.

Sponsorship

It's not all 'fun in the sun' when it comes to sponsorship — this lot covers the bad bits.
If you're doing the Edexcel or WJEC courses you can skip this page too.

Sponsorship Isn't All Great Though

1) It could all turn nasty — get injured, lose your form or get a bad reputation and it's bye–bye sponsorship deal.

2) Abuse of power — associating cigarettes and alcohol with sport gives a false image of health.

3) Sometimes athletes have to fulfil contracts with their sponsor — they might have to turn up at a special event or appear in a TV advert (even if they don't want to).

4) Athletes can get into trouble with their sponsor if they're photographed using another company's products.

It's Not Always Easy to get Sponsored

Companies don't always want to take a chance on people who are new to a sport — they want to know they're putting their name on someone good. And if a team or sportsperson can't find a sponsor, they might not be able to compete.

1) Big companies want people to see their logos — so they won't bother with small, local teams or sports with a low profile. High profile sports (like football) usually find it quite easy to get sponsored.

2) When games are going to be broadcast on TV, sponsors are keen to be associated with them, but often won't sponsor non-televised games.

3) Local teams and leagues are more likely to be sponsored by local companies, who want to get their name seen by the community. There can be lots of teams competing for sponsorship though, and not all of them will be lucky. They have to send out lots of begging letters asking for sponsorship.

4) Sometimes school teams get sponsored by companies whose owners have children in the team. This is good while it lasts, but the sponsorship might suddenly disappear when the child leaves. It might also mean that the team feels obliged to include the child in the team, even if there are better players — it could lead to favouritism.

5) If teams rely on sponsors from previous years or events, they could be left in a bit of a pickle if the sponsors change their minds.

Some Types of Sponsorship are Unacceptable

1) Cigarette and tobacco companies aren't allowed to sponsor sports in the EU — cigarettes are harmful, so they can't be promoted through sport.

2) Alcoholic drinks companies can sometimes be sponsors, though not usually for youth events.

3) Companies that are considered by many to promote racist, sexist or other discriminatory views aren't allowed to be sponsors.

4) Unhealthy food companies have to be careful when they sponsor sports — they can't suggest that their products are healthy (because they're associated with sports) if they're not.

5) Companies like banks, sports clothes/equipment brands and car manufacturers don't normally have any problems being sponsors.

You're probably so used to seeing sponsors' names on things, you hardly even realise they're there — like Barclays Premier League, or the Reebok Stadium. It's important you know the downsides to sponsorship — make sure you know what types are unacceptable, and why some teams struggle to find sponsors.

   *Sorry, I couldn't find a sponsor for this page

International Sport

International competitions were first organised in the 19th century — and since then they've just got bigger and bigger. Learn about their pros and cons, and how attitudes towards them vary. If you're doing a WJEC or Edexcel course you don't need to know about this for the exam — so hop, skip and jump on to the next page.

There are Loads of International Sporting Events

These include:

THE OLYMPIC GAMES: Summer and winter competitions held every four years.

THE PAN AMERICAN GAMES: Held every four years for countries in North, South or Central America.

THE COMMONWEALTH GAMES: Held every four years for countries in the Commonwealth (a group of countries that used to be in the British Empire).

WORLD CUPS: In many sports, e.g. cricket, rugby, football — every four years.

Nowadays, nearly every major sport has its own world championship.

Big International Competitions have Pros and Cons

Big tournaments sound great, and mostly they are. But, as always, there are some downsides.

BENEFITS

1) Players and supporters from different countries can meet, and experience different cultures and ways of life.

2) Competition between the best athletes in the world constantly pushes standards higher.

3) International events encourage people from all around the world to take part in sport.

PROBLEMS

1) Big tournaments are expensive to organise, so poor countries can't afford to stage them.

2) Not even rich countries are willing to host big competitions without help from big business — this makes sport more commercialised.

3) Some countries want success at sport to 'prove' they are more successful than an enemy. The USA and USSR used to do this.

Different Countries have Different Attitudes to Sport

Every country wants success in sport — it gives status and pride, and provides role models that will encourage people to be healthier. Different countries promote sport in different ways...

UNITED KINGDOM

1) PE is compulsory in schools.

2) Grants and sponsorship are available for promising talent.

3) Some top competitors have trust funds.

4) Various campaigns boost participation (see p60-62).

USA

1) PE is compulsory in schools.

2) School and college sport is high profile and attracts big sponsorship.

3) Scholarship schemes help promising athletes.

4) Top college athletes go into professional leagues.

FORMER EASTERN BLOC (Countries that were dominated by the USSR)

1) Sport was controlled by the state.

2) Talented children were trained from a very young age — then given token jobs in the army or industry.

3) Sport has been more open since 1989.

THIRD WORLD COUNTRIES

1) Popular sport has to be cheap — football and athletics are booming.

2) International success will earn money.

3) Athletes are often given token government jobs.

The third international water fight was a great success...

There's quite a lot here again. You won't really need to know much about individual competitions — just as long as you know they exist and can name a few of them. The most important bits are the benefits of them, along with the problems they cause — so spend a bit more time on these.

International Sport

The first ever Olympic Games were held in 776 BC in Ancient Greece and they've changed quite a bit since then. If you're doing the Edexcel or WJEC courses you can miss this page and hop straight over to media.

Olympic Organisations Keep Things Fair

1) The International Olympic Committee (IOC) is made up of members from just about all the countries that compete. They make judgements and rules to keep things fair. They also decide where the Olympics are going to be held. It's their job to promote the Olympics and the Olympic spirit (the Olympic spirit is believing it's more important to take part than win).

2) The British Olympic Association (BOA) looks after the UK's involvement in the Games. It selects athletes for 'Team GB' and helps them to prepare, e.g. by organising time management and goal setting workshops.

Being a Host City has its Good and Bad Points

The Olympics are always hosted by a city, not a whole country.
Hosting the Games should bring only advantages — but it doesn't always work out like that...

ADVANTAGES

1) The host city gets added prestige — useful if you want to attract trade and tourism.
2) The facilities built for the Games can be used by the locals after the events have finished.
3) Businesses in the host city will do masses of extra trade during the Games.
4) The organisers can try to make a profit.

DISADVANTAGES

1) It's getting more expensive to host the Games.
2) If there are problems, the organisers could lose enormous amounts of money.
3) Security could be a problem — hooligans or terrorists might disrupt the Games.
4) If a city's infrastructure (e.g. its phone or transport systems) can't cope, it could lead to frustration for locals and visitors.

The Olympic Games have had Their Ups and Downs

Since the Modern Olympics started in 1896, there have been quite a few ups and downs.

1896 in ATHENS — The first Modern Olympic Games were organised by Baron de Coubertin. Only men could compete.

1936 in BERLIN — Hitler wanted the Games to prove the superiority of white northern Europeans. But the star of the games was Jesse Owens, a black American who won four golds.

1972 in MUNICH — Palestinian terrorists killed two, and kidnapped nine, Israeli athletes. The hostages, five terrorists and a policeman were later killed in a failed rescue attempt.

1980 in MOSCOW — The USA and many other countries boycotted the Games (i.e. they didn't go to them) as a protest against the Soviet invasion of Afghanistan.

1984 in LOS ANGELES — The Games made a big profit — most things were sponsored by large companies. The USSR and allies boycotted the games in retaliation for the 1980 American boycott.

1992 in BARCELONA — No boycotts, and South Africa entered a team for the first time since 1960. It had been banned since 1964 because of its racist apartheid laws.

2008 in BEIJING — There were some protests over China's human rights record, but the Games went quite smoothly.

I want to see hula-hooping in London 2012...

The Olympics are a massive deal, especially to the host city. They take years of preparation, and cost a lot of money. Make sure you can list all the advantages and disadvantages of hosting the Olympics.

Sport and the Media

You _can't avoid sport_ — it's there in the _daily papers_, on the _radio_, in _books_, in _films_, on the _Internet_.
Choose any type of _media_ and it's there. Which is great if you _love_ it, but not so great if it _bores_ you to tears.

Sport turns up _Everywhere_

1) _TV_ and _Radio_ — most _major sporting events_ will be shown on TV (_Wimbledon_ takes over
for two weeks every summer, and the _football World Cup_ is almost unavoidable).

2) _Cable_ and _Satellite_ — they provide _special TV channels_ dedicated to sport,
and sometimes show events on a _pay-per-view_ basis.

3) _Interactive TV services_ — you can find out _results_ and watch _extra coverage_ on these.

4) _Internet_ — there are some events you can watch _live_ (or get _live commentaries_ for)
on the internet. Big teams, sports organisations and tournaments will have their
own _websites_, so you can keep up-to-date with all their _news_.

5) _Newspapers_ and _Magazines_ — just about all newspapers have a _sports
section_, with _recent results_, _league tables_ and _general sporty news_.
You can also buy magazines _dedicated_ to _particular sports_.

6) _Books_ and _Films_ — examples include _biographies_ about sports
personalities, _coaching books_ for particular sports, and films such
as 'Million Dollar Baby' (which, if you've not seen it, is about boxing).

The media coverage of sport relies heavily on _technology_ (see p71). Apart from making all these
forms of coverage possible, it also improves them with things like _instant replays_, _photo finishes_,
underwater cameras, _split times_, and timing to hundredths or _thousandths of seconds_.

Media Coverage Can Be _Entertaining_ or _Informative_

SPORTS PROGRAMMES:
Can be for _entertainment_ (like live sport, highlights
or quiz shows) or _information_ (like documentaries).

You can also get _instructive_ or _educational_ programmes,
like a coaching series — such as 'Steve Smith's Guide
to Better Tiddlywinks'.

SPORTS ARTICLES:
Sports results and analysis (_informative_),
behind the scenes, players' private lives,
biographies (_entertainment_).

The _Director_ can _Influence_ the _Coverage_

1) The _director_ of a sports programme can _influence_ your _opinions_ of a sport or sportsperson.

2) Some sports can be _advertised_ to make them look really _exciting_ (like using _dramatic sound effects_
and _voice-overs_). _Attractive stars_ can also make you want to watch a particular sport.

3) The director _chooses_ which bits you see — and also which bits you _don't_. If they only show the
reaction to something, and not the _incident_ that led up to it, you could form a different _judgement_
than if you saw the whole thing.

4) It's possible to _edit interviews_, to make the person being interviewed come across in a _different light_
— the interviewee could appear _more arrogant_ or _less intelligent_ than they actually are.

I want to see the director's cut of Wimbledon...

Make sure you know the _different forms_ of _media_, and how they can show sports. _Beware_ of what you
see on TV — remember that the _director_ is _controlling_ what you see. He could even be _brainwashing_ you
into learning a new and obscure _sport_ or joining a secret snooker _cult_. Don't say I didn't warn you.

Sport and the Media

The <u>media</u> has lots of <u>influences</u> on modern sport — some of them are <u>good</u>, others are <u>bad</u>. You need to be able to give examples of both, and know how fashion affects sport too.

The <u>Media</u> can have a <u>Good Effect</u> on Sport...

The coverage of sport in the media does good stuff for sport.

The media: bringing sport & inspiration.

<u>Money</u> — Media companies pay for the rights to show a sport — <u>sponsorship</u> for a sport will also <u>increase dramatically</u> if it's popularised by the media.

<u>Education</u> — People learn about the <u>rules and tactics</u> of sports.

<u>David Beckham</u> — (OK I couldn't think of a good 'D'). Produces <u>role models</u> for people to aspire to. If the role models stay good, everything's fine.

<u>Inspiration</u> — Brings sport to people who may not experience it otherwise. This can <u>encourage participation</u>.

<u>Aid to Coaching</u> — Sport on TV and video lets you <u>study the performance</u> of others.

<u>Promotional campaigns</u> in the media can also <u>encourage</u> people to <u>take up sports</u> and have a <u>healthy</u>, <u>active</u> <u>lifestyle</u>. Just before, during and after <u>Wimbledon</u>, lots of <u>tennis centres</u> run sessions to try and get <u>children</u> involved. Campaigns also use <u>famous sports stars</u> as <u>role models</u> to make children want to take up sports.

...and a <u>Bad Effect</u> on Sport

The media does lots of good for sport, but it has a <u>dark side</u> to it tooooooo....(that was supposed to sound eerie).

<u>Bias</u> — Only the really popular spectator sports get plenty of coverage. Very <u>little coverage</u> is given to <u>less popular sports</u>, starving them of all the benefits shown above.

<u>Lack of attendance</u> — Watching it live on telly means you're not at the game — <u>reducing ticket sales</u>, then the media 'steals' more of this money with 'pay-per-view' or channel subscription fees.

<u>Overload</u> — <u>too much sport</u> (according to some people).

<u>Open season</u> — <u>Sports stars are hounded</u> by the media, who are quick to pounce if a sports superstar's halo slips.

<u>Demands</u> — The media actually <u>imposes</u> rules on sports to make them <u>more exciting</u>, e.g. tie breaks were introduced into tennis, partly as a result of <u>media pressure</u> to make matches shorter.

The sinister face of the media.

Sports can go <u>In</u> and <u>Out</u> of <u>Fashion</u>

1) Sports or leisure activities can go <u>in</u> or <u>out</u> of <u>fashion</u>. In the 90s, aerobics became very fashionable with endless tedious celebrity fitness videos being released.

2) Sports clothing has also become a lot more fashionable. If the <u>clothing</u> or <u>equipment</u> for a physical activity is fashionable, people are more likely to do the activity.

3) Going to the <u>gym</u> is very fashionable at the moment — which has meant more gyms have opened — so people now have <u>more opportunity</u> to go to them.

Shopping — a very fashionable sport...

Like with sponsorship (see p65-66), the media's involvement in sport isn't just a bed of roses. Learn what things sport <u>relies</u> on the media for, but know how it <u>suffers</u> from media coverage as well.

Technology in Sport

If you're doing the AQA or WJEC courses, you need to need know how advances in <u>science</u> and <u>technology</u> have affected sport. Some developments help athletes <u>improve</u> their <u>performance</u>, while others help keep things <u>fair</u>.

Technology helps Athletes Improve

1) Lots of the <u>technology</u> used today is designed to help athletes <u>perform better</u> at their sports.
2) <u>New materials</u> are used to make sports <u>equipment</u> and <u>clothes</u> more <u>effective</u> — from <u>shoes</u> to <u>swimming costumes</u> to <u>tennis rackets</u>.
3) Athletes' <u>diets</u> can be designed to <u>enhance</u> their performance, due to a better <u>scientific understanding</u> of what their bodies <u>need</u> to do well.
4) <u>Improvements</u> to <u>training facilities</u> like <u>all-weather pitches</u> make sport more <u>accessible</u> for everyone. <u>Roofs</u> on <u>stadiums</u> (like Centre Court at Wimbledon) mean that matches can go ahead even if it <u>rains</u> (which, let's face it, it probably will).
5) There have also been developments to make sports <u>safer</u>.

ICT can be used in Training

1) <u>ICT programs</u> can be used to <u>analyse</u>, <u>monitor</u> and <u>plan</u> training sessions.
2) Sometimes <u>coaches</u> will make <u>videos</u> of their athletes' training so the athletes can see for themselves how they need to <u>improve</u>. Videos can also be used to <u>track progress</u>.
3) Computer software lets you analyse <u>performance</u> and <u>training statistics</u> — things like <u>service speeds</u> in <u>tennis</u> and <u>golf swings</u>. A training programme can be <u>designed</u> around the <u>results</u> of the analysis so the athlete can work on <u>weak areas</u>.

4) Better technology has led to more <u>accurate timings</u> in events like <u>sprints</u> and <u>cycle races</u> — they can be measured to tiny <u>fractions</u> of a <u>second</u>, so <u>minute improvements</u> are noticed.
5) <u>Interactive software</u> (even things like <u>games consoles</u>) can be used in training, especially in <u>bad weather</u>.

Some Technology helps the Referee or Umpire

<u>Referees</u> and <u>umpires</u> have to make lots of <u>snap decisions</u> in <u>live matches</u>. Sometime it can be hard to <u>judge</u>, especially if they're far away from the action. Technological developments like the <u>video official</u>, <u>replays</u> and <u>photo finishes</u> help them make <u>fair judgments</u>.

<u>CYCLOPS</u> (<u>tennis</u>) — Cyclops is a system used at <u>Wimbledon</u> to help decide if <u>serves</u> are <u>in</u> or <u>out</u>. It's made up of <u>infrared beams</u> that lie just above the ground. If the beams are <u>broken</u> (if a serve is <u>out</u>), they make a '<u>beep</u>'. It can make <u>mistakes</u> — but it's pretty <u>accurate</u>, and makes things a lot <u>easier</u> for the umpire (especially if the balls are travelling at over 140 mph). It's also used at big championships like the <u>US Open</u> and the <u>Australian Open</u>.

<u>HAWK-EYE</u> (<u>cricket</u> and <u>tennis</u>) — Hawk-Eye was originally developed for <u>cricket matches</u>, but has since been used in <u>tennis matches</u> as well. It uses a set of <u>six cameras</u> to <u>track</u> and <u>predict</u> the path of the <u>ball</u>. In cricket, it's mainly used by the <u>commentators</u> to discuss the umpire's <u>lbw</u> (leg before wicket) <u>decisions</u>. In tennis, it's used for the players to <u>challenge</u> the decision of whether their shots are in or out.

I say — that's simply not cricket...

The <u>lbw</u> (leg before wicket) rule in <u>cricket</u> is a bit confusing — it's when the <u>umpire</u> decides that the ball would have hit the <u>stumps</u> (and so got the batter <u>out</u>) if the batter hadn't got in the <u>way</u> of the ball. It's normally down to the <u>umpire's decision</u>, but technology like <u>Hawk-Eye</u> can confirm whether he's right.

Revision Summary — Section Five

Congratulations! You've made it to the end of the book. Well, there's still just a little bit of exam advice on the next few pages, but this is the end of all the stuff you have to learn. Make sure you can answer all these questions before you go off and make yourself a celebratory cup of tea. You've earned it.

1) What's leisure time? What's recreation?
2) Give three reasons why people have more leisure time.
3) What's the difference between public sector facilities and private sector facilities?
4) Name six factors that affect the sports we choose, and explain why.
5) Explain how your family can influence which sports you do.
6) How might your religion affect the sports you do?
7) Name four problems facing women's sport today.
8) Name three things the Women's Sports Foundation does.
9) How can your age affect which physical activities you do?
10) Give an example of a type of exercise that is good for asthma sufferers.
11) Name two disabled role models.
12) Give three ways a good PE teacher can affect your attitude towards PE.
13) Give three advantages of schools forming links with sports clubs.
14) Give four ways, other than actually playing, that you could get involved in sport.
15) Outline the key requirements of the Healthy Schools policy.
16) What do PESSCL and PESSYP stand for?
17) Describe a) Specialist Sports Colleges, b) Gifted and Talented Programmes and c) School Sport Partnerships.
18) What is the 'Five Hour Offer'?
19) What does Sport England do? What's 'Start, Stay, Succeed' all about?
20) Name three different programmes that the Youth Sport Trust is involved in. Explain what each one does.
21) Name and describe the three main types of competition.
22) What's the difference between a professional and an amateur?
23) Give five ways that amateurs can get the money to afford to train full time.
24) Name three possible sports-related careers (other than being a professional athlete).
25) Give three ways sponsorship can be good for sport.
26) Name four things sponsors get out of sponsorship.
27) Give three ways sponsorship can be bad for sport.
28) Give two types of sponsorship that are unacceptable.
29) Name three international sporting events.
30) Describe the advantages and disadvantages of hosting the Olympics.
31) Name four different types of media that feature sport.
32) Describe the good and bad effects the media has on sport.
33) How is ICT used in training sessions?
34) Describe Cyclops and Hawk-Eye.

Answering Exam Questions

Hurray — you made it to the end of the book. Now there's just the <u>tiny</u> matter (ahem) of the exam left. Here's what to <u>expect</u> in your exam and some <u>exam tips</u> to help you on your way to GCSE PE victory.

In the Exam — Read the Questions and Don't Panic

1) <u>Read</u> every question <u>carefully</u>.

2) The <u>number of marks</u> each question is worth is shown in <u>brackets</u> like this:

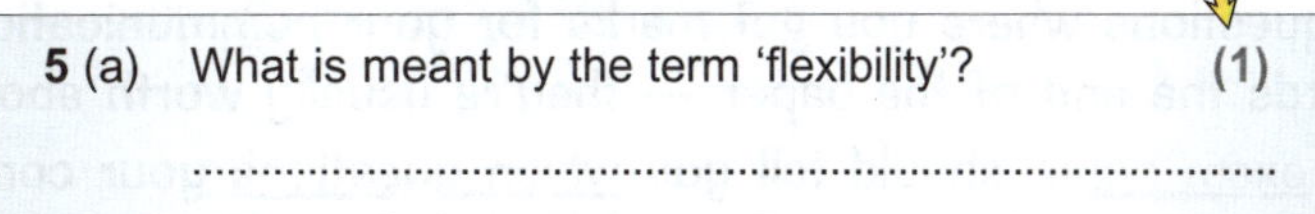

3) The number of marks is normally a <u>good guide</u> to the <u>number of points</u> you need to make in your answer.

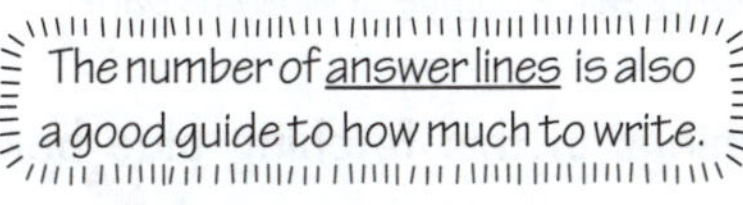

4) It also helps you know roughly <u>how long</u> to spend on a question — you don't want to use half an hour writing an essay for one mark.

5) Make sure your answers are <u>clear</u> and <u>easy to read</u>. If the examiner can't read your handwriting, they won't be able to give you any marks.

6) <u>Don't panic</u> — if you get stuck on a question, just <u>move on</u> to the next one. You can come back to it if you have time at the end.

Your Exam is Made up of Different Types of Question

Multiple Choice

1) The multiple choice questions will give you a choice of <u>four</u> or <u>five</u> possible answers.

   It tells you on the paper how to answer the question — you'll either have to <u>circle</u> the answer, or put a <u>tick</u> or a <u>cross</u> in a <u>box</u>.

2) Make sure you only choose <u>one</u> answer — if you pick more than one, you won't get any marks.

   (Don't worry if you make a mistake though — you can change your answer, as long as it's clear which one you've gone for in the end.)

3) If you <u>don't know</u> the answer to a question, <u>guess</u>. You don't lose marks for a wrong answer — and if you guess, you've at least got a chance of getting it right.

Short and Long Answer Questions

1) <u>Short answer</u> questions are usually worth between <u>one</u> and <u>four</u> marks. <u>Long answer</u> questions are normally worth about <u>six</u> marks.

2) Make sure you <u>read the question</u> carefully. For example, if you're asked for two influences, make sure that you give <u>two</u>, otherwise you won't get all the marks.

Questions on a Scenario You Were Given Before the Exam ...but only if you're doing AQA

1) If you are doing AQA, you'll be given a copy of a <u>scenario</u> a few weeks before the exam.

   This is basically just a <u>story</u> about someone doing some kind of <u>physical activity</u> (or perhaps someone doing no exercise at all...).

2) <u>Read through</u> the scenario <u>really carefully</u>. Have a good think about the <u>issues</u> it raises — things like what kind of <u>training</u> the person in the story might need to do, or how they could improve their <u>diet</u>.

3) The scenario will be printed out for you in the exam paper. You'll be asked a mixture of <u>short</u> and <u>long answer</u> questions about it. Use everything you thought about <u>beforehand</u> to help you answer.

Don't panic — now where's my towel...

So — <u>read</u> the question, look at the number of <u>marks</u>, answer the question and <u>don't panic</u>. Make sure that you sleep and eat well the night before the exam, so you're in tip top condition for the big day.

Answering Exam Questions

It's not just PE those examiners want to test you on, oh no. They've included a few marks for how well you can <u>communicate</u> your answer. It sounds tricky, but if you take care it could mean some easy marks.

Don't Forget to Watch Your Spelling and Grammar

1) Some of the questions on the exam paper will test your <u>written communication skills</u> (otherwise known as '<u>how well you can write your answer</u>') as well as your amazing **PE** knowledge.

2) The questions where you get marks for your communication skills will always be the <u>longer ones</u> towards the end of the paper — they're usually worth about <u>6 marks</u> each.

3) Your <u>exam paper</u> should tell you <u>which questions</u> your communication skills are being tested on.
   AQA and WJEC stick a <u>list</u> on the <u>front cover</u>. Edexcel and OCR put an <u>asterisk</u> (*) next to the <u>question number</u> inside the paper. AQA also mark these questions with 'Answer in continuous prose'.

4) You can pick up some easy marks just by making sure that you do the things in this fetching blue box.

> 1) Make sure you <u>answer the question</u> being asked — it's dead easy to go off on a tangent.
> 2) Make sure your answer is <u>organised</u>. It's a really good idea to have a think what you're going to cover in your answer before you start writing it. That way you can make sure you <u>structure</u> your answer well, and cover all the points you want to.
> 3) Write in <u>full sentences</u> and use correct <u>spelling</u>, <u>grammar</u> and <u>punctuation</u>.
> 4) Use the correct <u>PE terminology</u>.

EXAMPLE

> **15*** A school wants to encourage its pupils to take more exercise outside of PE lessons.
> Discuss the factors that may affect a teenager's participation in extra-curricular physical activity.　　(6)

Good answer

There are lots of factors that might affect a teenager's level of participation in extra-curricular physical activity. Some of these factors are practical, and others are social.

Participation may be limited by the availability of sports facilities in the local area. Access to facilities may be limited by local transport.

Cost may be a factor. If joining a sports club or buying equipment is too expensive, it will discourage people from taking part.

If the teachers at a school encourage pupils to take part in sports, and the school provides a variety of extra-curricular sports clubs, this may encourage pupils to participate.

A teenager's peer group can have a big influence on their choice of extra-curricular activities. If a certain sport is fashionable amongst your peers, it may encourage you to take part in that activity too.

Gender may also have an effect on which sports people take part in. Some sports are seen as traditionally 'male' or 'female'. For example, if the school started a netball club, it may find it easier to encourage girls to participate than boys.

Having an appropriate sporting role model might encourage a teenager to participate in sport. This may be a family member, like a parent, or a role model from the media, such as a famous footballer.

Bad Answer

<u>Things which might encourage participation in sport:</u>
- good local facilities
- local transport available
- encouragement by teachers/school
- sport being popular in your peer group
- sporting role models

<u>Things which might stop teenagers participating in sport:</u>
- cost
- bad local facilities
- gender — if only traditionally 'male' or 'female' sports are available.

There's nothing wrong with the PE in the bad answer, but you'd miss out on some nice easy marks just for not bothering to link your thoughts together properly or put your answer into proper sentences.

For easy marks — communicate well good...

So for the <u>long answer</u> questions, write in <u>full sentences</u> and watch your <u>spelling</u> and <u>grammar</u>.
<u>Organise</u> what you want to say <u>before</u> you start writing, and those marks could be yours for the taking.

Index

Index